More Ripples from Warwickshire's Past

PAUL BOLITHO

To my wife, Doreen, who not only took most of the photographs and read the proofs, but helped and encouraged me all through to publication.

Copyright © Paul Bolitho, 1997
Published by the author,
17 Oken Court,
Warwick,
CV34 4DF
Tel: (01926) 401301

Printed and bound by Warwick Printing Company Limited,
Theatre Street, Warwick CV34 4DR

ISBN

British Library Cataloguing-in-Publication Data
Bolitho, Paul
    More Ripples from Warwickshire's Past
    1. Social Life, history
    I. Title
    920.04248

Contents

Preface

THE success of "Ripples from Warwickshire's Past" and the interest shown in local history generally prompts me to publish a further collection of stories of Warwickshire men and women who have left their mark upon the national scene. This selection is not intended to be in any way comprehensive, but it shows that the county has produced many more people of note than Shakespeare and George Eliot.

Paul Bolitho

— 1 —

Cave Dwelling Bishop

U NTIL quite recently there was no Bishop of Warwick, but 1,400 years ago there was one! Tradition has it that in the sixth century the monk St. Dubritius arrived from the Wye valley bearing the Christian message to the Britons who lived around the stronghold above the River Avon where Warwick Castle now stands. He is said to have established his episcopal seat in a church which he dedicated in honour of All Saints, later to be enclosed by the walls of the Norman castle. When he felt harassed he secluded himself in a cave at Guy's Cliffe – long before it was named after the tenth century hero – and there he founded an oratory dedicated to St. Mary Magdalene. Later he became Bishop of Llandaff, and his longing for solitude led him later still to move further westwards to the very tip of Wales. David succeeded him as Bishop there, and Dubritius finally retired to Bardsey, the Isle of Saints, off the North Wales coast where he died in 612. His bones were transferred as relics to Llandaff Cathedral when it was rebuilt in the 1120s. After such a long journey it was thought desirable to wash the bones, but the water bubbled as though a red hot stone had been plunged into it! This was taken as a sign that the holy dust of Bardsey should be allowed to remain, and the relics were wrapped in linen as they were and enshrined in the chapel of St. Mary in the north aisle of the cathedral. Dubritius, or Dyfrig to the Welsh, is regarded as one of the three patron saints of the cathedral.

These traditions may be somewhat legendary but they do mean that Christianity – Celtic Christianity – was established in Warwickshire considerably before Augustine introduced, or rather re-introduced, Roman Christianity into these islands in 597.

When Roger of Newburgh, Earl of Warwick, completed the building of the Norman St. Mary's in 1123, Dubritius's church of All Saints was still standing in the castle precincts, and he then incorporated it into St. Mary's parish.

Seven centuries later when the Victorian church was built at Emscote in 1854 – 56, the All Saints name of the church of St. Dubritius was perpetuated, and a mission hall was dedicated to him in nearby Pickard Street. Alas, although a handsome new church has now been erected in place of the old building, the commemoration of Dubritius in window, fresco and reredos is there no more. However, at the time an enterprising

Effigy of St. Dubritius at Salford Priors.

vicar rescued from demolition an effigy of Dubritius which stood above the south door of the Victorian church. This effigy now stands in a niche of the beacon tower of Salford Priors Church. The robed priest holds two pastoral crooks and a crozier in his left hand and his right hand is held in blessing. The crooks may stand for Warwick and Llandaff. Less plausibly it has been suggested that the crozier stands for Caerleon, because Geoffrey of Monmouth – writing long afterwards in the twelfth century – states that Dubritius was Archbishop of Caerleon ("the fort of the legion") who supposedly crowned King Arthur. On the other hand Warwick was called Caerleon ("the fort of Earl Guthleon") in Dubritius's day.

Dubritius figures in Tennyson's "Idylls of the King" as "Dubric the high saint, chief of the Church in Britain." A penitent is made to say in "Enid and Geraint":-

"And oft I talked with Dubric, the high saint,
Who, with mild heat of holy oratory,
Subdued me somewhat to that gentleness,
Which, when it weds with manhood, makes a man."

— 2 —

The Lady of the Mercians

WE owe Warwick to Ethelfleda, the Lady of the Mercians, who restored the ravaged Saxon town and built her burh there in 914 on rising ground above the river as part of a defensive system against the marauding Vikings. This burh was not just a castle merely to protect its lord and his retainers, but a fortified town to protect the whole population of the area. It is commemorated in the Castle grounds by Ethelfleda's Mound.

Ethelfleda was the eldest daughter of King Alfred and Queen Elswith. In 884 when she was fifteen, her father gave her in marriage to Ethelred, a scion of the old Mercian royal house. The Anglo-Saxon Chronicle concentrates on Wessex, but while Alfred was gaining his spectacular victories, Ethelred was unobtrusively recapturing western Mercia from the Danes, and as ealdorman accepted the overlordship of Alfred. The marriage was politically important because it led to the completion of the union of Mercia with Wessex under the West Saxon kings, the nucleus of a united England. Before Alfred's death in 899 the joint rule of Ethelred and Ethelfleda had established burhs at Worcester, Gloucester and Hereford. They built Shrewsbury in 901 and further strengthened Mercia against the Danes by fortifying and colonising the ruined Roman city of Chester in 907, thereby cutting off the Norsemen of Ireland and Wales from those in the Danelaw. After the death of Ethelred in 911 Ethelfleda set herself to secure Mercia against further attacks by the Danes by building more burhs which would hinder them from entering the country either from North Wales or the North East. Firstly in 912 she set about the defence of the middle course of the Severn by building, for example, a fortress at Bridgnorth. In 913 she raised two fortresses on the Watling Street boundary between England and the Danelaw – at Tamworth and at Stafford. Then in 914 she barred invaders using the Fosse Way and commanded the River Avon by her celebrated burh at Warwick. She had further victories in battle on either side of her beloved Mercia -- over the Welsh at Brecknock and over the Danes at Derby. The Danes of Leicester submitted peaceably, and even the Danes of York promised to accept her rule and agreed to obey her.

This chip off the old block, Alfred's daughter, died at her palace at Tamworth on June 12th 918 and was buried beside her husband in

St. Oswald's, Gloucester. Although overshadowed in the history books by her father Alfred, her brother Edward the Elder and her nephew Athelstan, Ethelfleda emerges as a reluctant but successful fighter who sought to civilise and live in peace with her Viking enemies.

— 3 —

Guy of Warwick, Hero and Hermit

E VERYBODY knows about King Arthur and Robin Hood, but how many people today are familiar with the story of Guy of Warwick, the third person in the trinity of our legendary national heroes? Well-known to earlier generations through chapbooks sold by pedlars and children's literature, Guy is hardly known today outside Warwickshire. Yet his stirring tales of chivalry rank alongside those of our other two champions.

Based, like Arthur and Robin, on a real person, Guy flourished during the reign of Ethelfleda's nephew King Athelstan (925 – 939). Like them also the rest of his exploits are almost wholly myth, stories handed down by word of mouth over hundreds of years. So that, because our earliest written account comes from the 13th century, our Saxon Guy, like Arthur, is conventionally portrayed in mediaeval armour. He must not, however, be confused with the 14th century Guy of Warwick who was responsible for the execution of Piers Gaveston, in spite of the fact that Guy's Cliffe and Blacklow Hill are so near to one another.

The legends concerning Guy have confusing variants, their sequence can be inconsistent, and the stories as a whole are not exactly in character, but Guy was said to have come from Wallingford and to be the son of Siward, the steward to Rohand, Earl of Warwick. So at first his courtship of the earl's daughter Felice (or Phyllis) was rejected because of his lowly position.

However Felice eventually returned his love. But, fearful lest her father might disapprove, she required him to perform deeds of valour to gain her hand. So he set off to the continent in search of adventure. Landing in Normandy he was just in time to save a fair lady condemned to be burnt alive on a false charge of perjury. From there he went on to a tournament where the prize was the hand in marriage of Blanche, the daughter of the Emperor of Germany. Nearly killing several of his rivals he triumphed over all the other knights, but declined the prize because of his love for Felice. On his return to Warwick, his prospective father-in-law was won over, but

5

Guy and the Wild Boar ('Slim Jim'), Coventry Road, Warwick.

Felice was more demanding: "The winning of a lady and her steed are but small things to what thou yet must do. I will ever love thee though thou never doest more, but cannot grant the use of love till then." Not exactly chivalrous on her part: perhaps Guy's subsequent rejection of Felice was poetic justice!

To the second part of Guy's quest belongs the story of the Dun Cow. This huge but originally placid beast, 12 feet high and 18 feet long, roamed Dunsmore Heath, now straddled by the A45 and M45. It had been milked dry (into a sieve instead of a pail!) by the greedy locals, and as a result had been turned into a raging monster, spreading destruction wherever it went. Guy found that an arrow could not pierce its hide and had to kill it with a battle-axe. For thus rescuing the people from their own folly Guy was knighted by the King, and the Dun Cow has entered public house nomenclature.

Guy also killed one dragon on the continent and another in the North of England. He also slew a wild boar on his continental travels – commemorated in a statue in Coventry Road in Warwick.

Back on the mainland of Europe, Guy was ambushed by some sixteen soldiers (legends are very specific!) in the pay of Duke Otto of Tuscany, one of the unsuccessful competitors in the German tournament, and he proceeded to kill most of them single-handed. He then went to the assistance of Duke Segyn of Louvain, an enemy of the emperor whose daughter he had rejected, and forced the combatants to make peace. He then set sail for Constantinople to fight the Saracens; repulsed a pirate fleet; killed the Sultan and brought his head back to camp as a trophy; declined to marry the daughter of the Duke of Burgundy (but only at the church!) because of his love for Felice; and finally slew his long time adversary Duke Otto in single combat.

Guy returned to England a second time to be accepted by Felice and they were married at long last. A month later his father-in-law died and Guy became Earl of Warwick. The couple had one son, Reinbrun, who eventually became Earl of Warwick in his turn.

Guy, however, was unhappy with his newly found pomp and wealth – and full of remorse for all the blood he had shed, even in just causes. "O, pardon me, just Heaven! I have done nothing yet thy grace to purchase, but spent my time about a woman's face; for beauty I have shed a world of blood, hating all others for one mortal creature." Poor Felice was taken aback, but chivalry notwithstanding, he now deserted her – almost for ever as it turned out. He must needs go abroad a third time, not now as a knight in shining armour, but as a penitent in pilgrim's garb, bound for the Holy Land to atone for his sins. A pilgrimage not without adventure: he killed the giant Amarant on the way.

When eventually the pilgrim returned to England incognito, it was to find the Danes before Winchester (an historical impossibility at that date) challenging King Athelstan to single combat to decide the issue. In spite of his contrition as a pilgrim and his failing health, Guy predictably resolved the situation by throwing off his palmer's weeds and killing the giant Colbrand in a David and Goliath encounter. This coup de grace to his heroic deeds saved his country. Guy's identity was then revealed and the King vowed, "In Warwick Castle shall thy sword be lodged."

Here the legend becomes even more incredible. If the king found out Guy's identity, why did Felice never do so, especially as she is said to have seen him kill Colbrand? One account says she did find out: he became her pensioner for fifteen years and every day he came to the gates of Warwick Castle, though not once in all that time did he speak to her other than as a holy hermit! Had he no thought for her feelings?

The more usual story says that Felice never recognised him. Guy reverted to his pilgrim's attire, withdrew to a cave at Guy's Cliffe on the banks of the Avon just north of the town and all those years regularly begged for the alms she distributed at the castle gates. Again our credibility is stretched because it is said that Felice would ask the begging palmers if they had been to the Holy Land and heard anything of her husband!

Then when Guy lay dying he sent Felice her ring via a herdsman; she hurried to him; and there in the cave they were reunited as he died. Felice died of a broken heart shortly afterwards. An addition to the legend says that she threw herself into the river at a spot illogically named Guy's Leap – a later accretion, since suicide had no place in the code of chivalry.

Centuries later the great earl Richard Beauchamp erected a chantry chapel at Guy's Cliffe for the repose of the souls of Guy and others of his supposed ancestors, and you can still see an eight foot high representation of our hero in situ.

N.B. "Guy's Sword" and "Guy's Porridge Pot" in Warwick Castle did not belong to Guy, but are of a much later date.

— 4 —

The Flower of Chivalry

T HE glory of the Collegiate Church of St. Mary, Warwick, is the magnificent Chapel of our Lady, otherwise known as the Beauchamp Chapel, wherein lies the gilded effigy of Richard Beauchamp, Earl of Warwick, on a chest of Purbeck marble. But of those who marvel at the tomb, how many know anything of the man, considered the epitome of chivalry, who willed this chantry chapel, twenty-one years in the building, so that priests could say masses there for his soul for ever?

The one thing most of us know about him we prefer to forget – his unchivalrous involvement in the burning of Joan of Arc. In fact responsibility for Joan's death ultimately rested with the English commander-in-chief, the Regent, the Duke of Bedford, rather than with the Earl of Warwick, as Bernard Shaw would have us believe. However, there is no doubt that Warwick wholeheartedly approved of her execution: it was in his castle at Rouen that Joan was kept a prisoner in terrible conditions and from which she was led to her cruel death.

Richard Beauchamp was, however, considered the ideal of knighthood. He had considerable success as a soldier and was the kind of personage his king would send on diplomatic missions. He was born in 1381, the son of Thomas Beauchamp II, an opponent of Richard II, and grandson of Thomas Beauchamp I, a hero of Crecy. So prominent was the family in the counsels of the state that the godfathers at his baptism were Richard II himself and a future Archbishop of Canterbury.

Richard succeeded as Earl of Warwick at the age of 20 on the death of his father in 1401. He put Owen Glendower to flight for Henry IV and then fought against Hotspur at the Battle of Shrewsbury in 1403. Between the years 1408 and 1410 he made a sort of mediaeval Grand Tour – a pilgrimage to the Holy Land via France and Italy, returning through Russia, Poland and Germany. Jousting en route was the order of the day, a much more dangerous pastime than present day sports: on one occasion Richard was on the point of killing his opponent outright when his host intervened, and on a later occasion – actually when attending the Church's Council of Constance as a lay representative! – he did kill his ducal adversary in a tournament before the Emperor.

The Beauchamp Tomb in the Chapel of Our Lady, St. Mary's, Warwick.

On his return to England Henry IV put Richard on the payroll of the Prince of Wales, and in 1413 he was Lord High Steward at the prince's coronation as Henry V. By 1415 he was Governor of Calais and present at the siege of Harfleur ("Once more unto the breach, dear friends..."), though he appears to have missed Agincourt escorting prisoners-of-war back to England. The following year he received the Emperor at Calais on behalf of the king. He was responsible for the capture of Rouen in 1419 and for the negotiations leading to the Treaty of Troyes in 1420 as a result of which Henry V married the French king's daughter Katherine. When the young king died two years later, so great was his confidence in the earl that he made him the guardian of his infant son, Henry VI, and it was in that capacity that Richard carried the lad to his coronation as King of England in Westminster Abbey in 1429, and then looked after him in Rouen Castle (with Joan in the dungeon) before his coronation in Paris as King of France in 1431.

Richard was later to become commander-in-chief in France, but by that time the English occupation of the country was becoming more and more tenuous, and he died at Rouen in April 1439 worn out by his labours.

Richard Beauchamp does not seem to have taken as much interest in Warwick Castle as, for example, his father Thomas who built Guy's Tower – he was away on the business of three successive sovereigns far too often – but he was responsible for the building of the chantry chapel at Guy's Cliffe, thereby fulfilling the wish of Henry V when he paid a visit to the town of Warwick a year before his death.

Interestingly, Richard's son and heir Henry became the first and only Duke of Warwick before he died at the age of only 22. Did Henry VI, one wonders, advance the son in the peerage because of gratitude for the care given to him by the father?

— 5 —

Morte D'Arthur

"So all day long the noise of battle roll'd
Among the mountains by the winter sea;
Until King Arthur's table, man by man,
Had fall'n in Lyonesse about their lord,
King Arthur."

Tennyson based his death of Arthur and his "Idylls of the King" on the fifteenth century "Morte D'Arthur" of Sir Thomas Malory. They are both stirring stuff, but legend, not history. Malory was writing nearly a thousand years after the Romano-British chieftain had defeated the Saxons at the Battle of Mount Badon in 516.

Malory's work is a pleasant jumble of Arthurian stories which he culled from the French romances of his day. He completed them in prison in 1469 or 1470 shortly before he died. The first printed edition was produced by Caxton in 1485.

The morality of the work has been questioned. Roger Ascham in his "Scholemaster" in 1568 denounced it as tending to immorality. "The whole pleasure of the book standeth in two special points, in open manslaughter and bold bawdry. In which book those be counted the noblest knights that do kill most men without any quarrel, and commit foulest adulteries by subtlest shifts: as Sir Lancelot with the wife of King Arthur his master and Sir Tristram with the wife of King Mark his uncle." But Malory condemns the scandals he deals with, and Caxton reckoned there was a moral to be drawn from the work: "Do after the good and leave the evil". Violent scenes are indeed essential to the story, but Malory also includes many noble acts of humanity and courtesy.

Sir Thomas Malory was lord of Newbold Revel near Brinklow, and I am sorry to say that he appears to have exemplified the darker side of so-called 'chivalry'. But then these "Ripples" seek to deal with the infamous as well as the famous. Born probably about 1416, he was too young, as has been previously thought, to have fought in the French wars with Richard Beauchamp, Earl of Warwick. He was certainly of age by 1439, and he was a respectable member of the country gentry in the 1440s, serving as an M.P. for Warwickshire. He was popularly supposed to have been imprisoned from 1451 simply for being on the wrong side in the subsequent Wars of the Roses, but at the beginning of the 1450s he suddenly began a career of spectacular crime, including the attempted murder of the Duke of Buckingham, sacrilegious robbery, rape and vandalism, which led the Lancastrian government to keep him in prison for the rest of the decade. He had connections with Warwick the Kingmaker, so he was freed when the Yorkists came to power in 1461. The early 1460s apparently mark a return to respectability, and in the winter of 1462 he helped Edward IV and the Kingmaker to besiege the Lancastrian castles of Alnwick, Bamburgh and Dunstanborough. But by the end of the decade when King and Kingmaker had fallen out, Malory was specifically excepted by name from Edward IV's general pardons and was in prison again. It was at this time that he completed "Morte D'Arthur", although he may have begun it during his earlier imprisonment. He died on March 14th 1471 and was buried in the Grey Friars near Newgate. He had concluded his book by asking his readers, "Pray for me while I am alive that God send me good deliverance, and when I am dead I pray you all pray for my soul."

— 6 —

The Kingmaker

APART from Bosworth, the Wars of the Roses (1455 – 1485) effectively ended with the Battle of Barnet in 1471, and in those sixteen years of strife one person stood out among all others – Warwick the Kingmaker. But to Tudor apologists he was merely part of the hurly-burly of the anarchy from which they had delivered England, the impression Shakespeare gives in the three parts of "Henry VI". So he sank into centuries of historical oblivion until 'rescued' firstly in the nineteenth century by Bulwer-Lytton's novel "The Last of the Barons" and by Charles Oman's "Life", more recently by Paul Kendall's sympathetic biography, and finally by the magnificent display in the undercroft of Warwick Castle.

Richard Neville was undoubtedly the most powerful territorial magnate of the fifteenth century. He was born in November 1428, the son of Richard Neville, shortly to become Earl of Salisbury, and his wife Alice, heiress of that earldom. His grandfather was Earl of Westmoreland whose vast estates in Durham and Yorkshire made him the rival of the Percies for dominance in the North. When he was only ten years old Richard was married to Anne, the daughter of Richard Beauchamp, Earl of Warwick. With the deaths of his brother-in-law Henry Beauchamp, Duke of Warwick, and Henry's young daughter in quick succession, he became Earl of Warwick in July 1449, thereby acquiring the Beauchamp estates and the estates of his mother-in-law. And when his father was killed at the Battle of Wakefield in 1460, he succeeded to the earldom of Salisbury and the great estates of Sheriff Hutton and Middleham in Yorkshire which were as much his headquarters as Warwick Castle. His authority was spread over more than half the counties of England!

These were the years of the anarchy of so-called bastard feudalism between Lancastrian and Yorkist factions, made possible by the weakness of the simple-minded, though pious, Henry VI, which was buttressed only by the determination of his queen, Margaret of Anjou. Magnates waged private wars to settle private scores; their bands of retainers were in effect private armies, none more so than those who sported the badge of the Bear and Ragged Staff. The age as a result became more ruthless, Richard included. He may have been brought up in the world of chivalry, but he was a merciless general rather than a courtly knight. No taking of prisoners was often the rule; execution of barons captured after battle was routine; and "Seek out the lords! Spare the commons!" was actually a merciful order!

The Earl of Warwick came into prominence in the early 1450s as the lieutenant of his uncle, Richard, Duke of York who was seeking to curb the misgovernment, or lack of government, of the Lancastrian advisers of Henry VI headed by the Duke of Somerset. When the King went temporarily insane in 1454, the threat of force was enough to instal York as Protector of the Realm, but when the King recovered the Lancastrians ousted York. At the resulting first battle of the Wars of the Roses in St. Albans in May 1455 – actually little more than a street scuffle – York owed his victory largely to Warwick's splitting the enemy forces in two.

In the subsequent distribution of offices among the Yorkists, Warwick was appointed to the important office of Captain of Calais, the only remaining English possession in France, strategically useful as either a springboard or a bolt-hole, especially as Warwick also had a fleet at his disposal. During an ensuing period of cold war, a determined Queen Margaret gained the upper hand again for the House of Lancaster, the King escaped from Yorkist tutelage, and Warwick survived an assassination attempt.

Open warfare again broke out in 1460. Warwick was victorious at the Battle of Northampton, ably assisted by his young cousin, York's son, Edward, Earl of March. The King was captured, being once more led back to London, and recognised the Duke of York as his successor. But then later in the year, unwisely refusing to wait for reinforcements, York was himself defeated and killed at Wakefield.

Our Earl heard of this disaster – in which he lost his father, a brother and a cousin as well as his uncle – at Warwick Castle. He immediately hastened to London. The disaster was also his opportunity to act as Kingmaker for his 19-year-old cousin Edward, the new Duke of York. Defeat, unusual for him, at the hands of the Queen's army at a second Battle of St. Albans in February 1461, decided him. It was useless trying to rouse men to keep on recapturing the puppet King Henry. If he could give men a new banner to rally to they could beat the Queen and her plundering horde. Warwick would produce another King, a better King.

When Warwick met Edward in the Cotswolds fresh from the young prince's victory at Mortimer's Cross on the Welsh border, Edward wanted to know where the King was. You are the King, Warwick told him. Edward readily agreed. They were able to march into London, and in March 1461 Edward IV was proclaimed King. Later that month Edward and his Kingmaker achieved complete victory at Towton in Yorkshire in the bloodiest battle of the whole war, the Lancastrians were scattered and the new Yorkist dynasty was secure.

Indolent and pleasure-loving, the new King was at first content to let Warwick run things for him. Besides subduing the remaining Lancastrian strongholds in the north, Warwick was allowed to conduct the

Government's foreign policy, and here he became a schemer par excellence. Though the Yorkists were friends of the Duke of Burgundy, Warwick favoured an alliance with the King of France who wished to destroy this over-mighty vassal and hinted that once that had been achieved perhaps Warwick, a kingmaker but not a sovereign himself, might like a continental appanage in the Low Countries. To this end it was suggested that Edward might marry a French princess, and, whilst asking for time to consider, the King did not show himself averse to the proposal. Yet imagine Warwick's consternation when the King subsequently announced to the Council that he had already married for love, one Elizabeth Woodville, a widow of no importance and a Lancastrian at that! For a start, it jeopardised the possibility of a French alliance. Worse still, the King had injured Warwick's pride, had made a fool of his Kingmaker before the world! And when he started showering honours on the new Queen's relations, the spectre arose of a House of Woodville to challenge the House of Neville. Little more than three years after Warwick had placed a new king on the throne the two men began to drift apart.

King and Kingmaker continued to pretend to be friends, but the Earl kept his distance either in Calais or in the Midlands and the North. He was convinced that a French alliance was necessary to forestall the possibility of a Lancastrian restoration by means of French arms. But while he was seeking such an alliance, Edward was negotiating behind his back with the Duke of Burgundy. In 1468 the King announced such a treaty which included the marriage of his sister to the Duke.

What was Warwick to do? He proceeded to win over the King's brother, the Duke of Clarence, and married his elder daughter Isabella to him. (The Kingmaker had no sons.) He could never be king himself, but if Clarence were king he would at least be the founding father of a new dynasty. At the same time the Earl stirred up trouble in the North under a certain Robin of Redesdale, and when the King marched north to quell this rebellion, Warwick and Clarence entered London. A royalist force was defeated in July 1469 at Edgcote, five miles north-east of Banbury, and at Olney the King found himself without a following. He was 'invited' by Warwick's brother, the Archbishop of York, to be escorted to his faithful liege, and the two men met at Coventry. The King was taken first to Warwick Castle and then to Middleham Castle, where he was treated with respect but left in no doubt as to who was master. He had to be made to see he could not rule without the man who had made him king, so Edward pretended to be ready to mend his ways. Unfortunately, the Kingmaker could not rule effectively either with the King a prisoner, and in the end, perhaps unwisely, he let him go.

Still maintaining outward amity with the King, Warwick next fomented a rising in Lincolnshire in March 1470 with the aim of putting the Duke of Clarence on the throne. But this time he had miscalculated: Edward triumphed, and Warwick and his family had to flee the country, poor Isabella giving birth to a dead child at sea.

But Warwick still had a second daughter Anne who might make him the grandfather of kings. If he could no longer rule through Edward and could not make Clarence king, there was a third – unthinkable – alternative. Or was it so unthinkable? Why not, through the proffered assistance of King Louis, make an alliance with his exiled archenemy, Queen Margaret, whom he had once called an adulterous bitch; dust off King Henry VI, now languishing in the Tower, and restore him to the throne; and marry Anne to their son, Edward, Prince of Wales? Incredibly, this is what actually happened. Warwick landed at Dartmouth; his Lancastrian-Neville army increased in numbers, while Edward's army suffered defections;

The Kingmaker in the Undercroft of Warwick Castle.

and so Edward fled the country embarking from Lynn for Burgundian territory. Henry VI became king once again, and for the few months from October 1470 to the Spring of 1471 the House of Lancaster once more 'ruled' England.

How long such a regime would have lasted from an economic point of view we do not know: the French alliance meant an embargo for English merchants on the lucrative trade with the Burgundian Low Countries. But politically a Neville-Lancastrian regime could not last. Indeed it collapsed even before Margaret arrived in England. In March 1471 Edward IV landed at Ravenspur at the mouth of the Humber with a mixed English and Burgundian force to regain his kingdom. The Kingmaker hurried from London to Warwick Castle where he prepared for the forthcoming battle, preparations so vividly portrayed in the present exhibition there. Then, safe behind the fortified walls of Coventry, he declined Edward's challenge to give battle as the Yorkists proceeded south, probably because he must have known that the Duke of Clarence, advancing from Banbury but feeling cheated by his father-in-law's latest intrigue, was about to play him false and switch sides again.

Edward then made a dash for London. The Earl of Warwick went after him, and then rashly, without waiting for Queen Margaret's reinforcements, gave battle. Edward came out from the capital, and on Easter Day 1471 the two sides met at Barnet – for all their supposed piety there was no Sunday observance! The fight could have gone either way. But a thick fog blanketing the field caused one body of Lancastrians to attack another by mistake, and panic followed. The Earl had decided to fight on foot to give heart to the common soldiers. In the retreat he lumbered back in his heavy armour to the horse-park, but, as he got his hand on the bridle of his horse, an enemy caught him from behind, hurled him to the ground, pulled up his visor and thrust a knife into his throat.

Shortly afterwards the restored King Edward put to death the inoffensive King Henry whom he had recaptured. Queen Margaret's invasion force was defeated at Tewkesbury, their son Prince Edward being slain on the field. So the main Lancastrian line on which the Kingmaker had so recently pinned his hopes was extinguished, and the Yorkist dynasty was secure for another fourteen years until Henry Tudor ended the strife once for all.

The Kingmaker's inheritance was divided between the Dukes of Clarence and Gloucester who succeeded to the ownership of Warwick Castle in turn. His Countess got nothing. As for his two daughters, Isabella mercifully died before her feckless husband Clarence was executed in 1478 for yet more plotting, the private execution giving rise to the story of his drowning in a butt of malmsey wine. Anne did indeed become a queen – of a sort. A year after her Lancastrian husband's death at Tewkesbury, she married the Yorkist Duke of Gloucester who later became Richard III – though, *pace* Shakespeare, he did not woo her over the dead husband's coffin. The daughters had been sacrificed to the relentless ambition of their father, Machiavelli's Prince, without a principality, fifty years before his time.

— 7 —

Saint of the Counter-Reformation

I N 1803 a French missionary priest came to Hampton-on-the-Hill just outside Warwick and in 1819 the Dormers, the local squires, built the first Roman Catholic church there. It was completed in 1830, the year after Catholic Emancipation. Charles, Lord Dormer dedicated it to his patron saint, Charles Borromeo, and Warwick Catholics came out from town to worship there until St. Mary Immaculate was built in West Street.

The Counter-Reformation of the late sixteenth century was the Roman Catholic answer to the Protestant Reformation. Just as Luther was originally opposed to the sale of indulgences rather to any belief in justification by works, so this was a reform of abuses rather than doctrine. And the strength of this movement at its best is seen in the work of St. Charles Borromeo, Cardinal Archbishop of Milan (1538 – 1584).

Borromeo was a nephew of Pope Pius IV, a beneficed clergyman at the age of 12, an archbishop at 21, a cardinal at 22, a devotee of hunting and a lover of splendour. But he experienced a colourful conversion. At the age of 25 he suddenly began to undertake the "Spiritual Exercises" of prayer recommended by St. Ignatius Loyola. He tried to resign most of the lucrative sinecure benefices he had amassed, and dismissed half his 150 servants, prescribing austere rules for the remainder. He lived on bread and water one day a week, used a scourge of spikes upon his body – and actually began to preach! That shook the members of his flock, because no one had ever heard of a cardinal preaching before!

Borromeo played an important part in the final session of the reforming Council of Trent (1562 – 63). He was responsible for the work of the Tridentine commission which drew up a revised catechism designed not for children or for those who could not read but for the parish clergy! This desire for an educated priesthood led him to establish six seminaries. And he also desired a wider educated public: he instituted an educational society which by the time of his death was controlling 740 schools. Orphanages and refuges for deserted wives were also founded through his zeal for pastoral care. He lived in Milan, the first archbishop to reside in the diocese for many years, and held synods of his clergy as required by the Council of Trent. Considered a model bishop, he regularly visited the thousand parishes in his diocese; he lived simply, and during a plague in 1576 – 78 won the admiration of all for the courageous care he gave to his flock. This reforming zeal met with opposition, including an assassination attempt. He died at a comparatively early age and was canonised only twenty-six years later.

If there had been more men like him half-a-century earlier there might have been no Reformation! Charles Dormer chose wisely in perpetuating his namesake at Hampton-on-the-Hill.

— 8 —

Master of the Hospital

T HOMAS Cartwright, a famous Puritan minister who sought to reform the Church of England from within, was the Master of the Lord Leycester Hospital in Warwick from 1585 until his death in 1603. Born in 1535, he was compelled to quit Cambridge during the reign of the Catholic Mary Tudor, but he returned on the accession of Elizabeth and, after a spell in Ireland, became Lady Margaret Professor of Divinity at the university in 1569. His sermons and lectures were popular and well-attended, but they were too critical of the government of the now Protestant Church establishment for the liking of the authorities, and he was deprived of his professorship in December 1570 and then of his college fellowship in the following September. He left England for Geneva, but returned in November 1572. However, he immediately engaged in more controversy and in December 1573 he fled to the continent to escape arrest, residing mainly in Antwerp for the next decade. Early in 1585 he returned to England again but was immediately thrown into the Fleet prison. However, he soon obtained his release, and towards the close of that year Robert Dudley, Earl of Leycester, took him under his wing and appointed him as the second Master of his newly-formed Hospital. Thereafter, apart from further imprisonment in the Fleet (1590 – 92) and a stay in Guernsey (1595 – 98), Cartwright remained in Warwick for the rest of his life.

His duties as Master required him to pray with the Brethren of the Hospital twice a day, catechise twice a week, and preach every Sunday in St. Mary's. Indeed it is recorded that he preached every Sunday morning in the 'lower parish' of Warwick (St. Nicholas) and every Sunday afternoon in the 'upper parish' (St. Mary's), and also lectured on Saturday afternoons in the 'upper church'. Ever the radical, at one time Cartwright was temporarily suspended by the bishop from preaching in the churches, but he continued to preach at the hospital and the public came to hear him there instead!

He also continued work on a translation of the New Testament which he had begun before he arrived in Warwick. The powers that be were in two minds about this. Secretary of State Walsingham sent him £100 to buy some books for his studies, but Archbishop Whitgift, fearful of

The Lord Leycester Hospital, Warwick.

controversies to which the publication of the work would probably give rise, persistently discouraged the undertaking and prohibited publication when a portion was ready for the press. Indeed the translation was not published until 1618, fifteen years after Cartwright's death.

How did he cram all this work and study into each day? He never discontinued the habit of early rising which he had begun in his youth – he used to get up at 2 a.m. or 3 a.m., or at the latest by 4 a.m!

The Mastership was worth £50 a year plus a house, to which Leycester added another £50. So for those days Cartwright was quite well off. On the other hand he was generous: it was his custom to distribute alms to the poor of Warwick on Sundays, and he likewise gave liberally to poor scholars and to people in prison. His life and influence were such that it was said, "There was not a nobleman or gentleman of quality in all the country that looked heavenward, or of any account for religious learning, but sought his company." And Dugdale says, "He was the first in the Church of England to pray extempore before the sermon"!

Thomas Cartwright died after a short illness at the Hospital on December 27th 1603, having preached on the Sunday before. He was buried in St. Mary's, but if there was ever any monumental record of him it must have perished in the Fire of 1694.

— 9 —

"Since there's no help, Come let us kiss and part..."

A FTER Shakespeare and George Eliot, Michael Drayton, the author of this famous sonnet, is Number Three in Warwickshire's pantheon of literature.

Drayton was born in March 1563 of yeoman stock in the village of Hartshill, near Nuneaton – according to local tradition in Chapel Cottage. At an early age he entered the household of Sir Henry Goodere of Polesworth, initially as a page, and attended the Abbey Gatehouse School there. Ralph Holinshed the chronicler lived nearby and undoubtedly encouraged young Drayton's love of learning.

In those days poetry was greatly esteemed in polite society. Courtiers, we know, dabbled in verse – Sir Philip Sidney, Lord Brooke and others. Less affluent aspiring poets like Drayton had to seek the patronage of the wealthy as tutors and secretaries and the like, and in return they would dedicate their verses to their patrons. That was usually the only way they could make ends meet. Drayton himself was to remain in one wealthy household or another all his life.

Though he also wrote for the stage, he was first and foremost a poet. His earliest work, "The Harmony of the Church", a metrical rendering of portions of the Scriptures, was published in 1591. For some unknown reason it offended the authorities and stocks were destroyed – a solitary copy remains in the British Library today.

In 1593 Drayton published "The Shepherd's Garland", with several parts and a chorus, casting himself in the role of 'Rowland of the Rock', a reference to Hartshill and the rock quarrying there. The following year he published fifty-one sonnets entitled "Idea's Mirror", addressed to Anne Goodere, the younger daughter of his first patron. He fell in love with the girl eight years his junior whom he had seen grow up. Though they remained friends, there is no evidence that she returned his love, and indeed the year after the sonnets came out she married another, a young squire named Henry Rainsford. Nevertheless for many years Drayton continued to sing her praises, and the final version of the poems which did not come out until 1619 contains the magnificent sonnet, "Since there's no help, come let us kiss and part".

In the search for patronage, no doubt the writers of the time could on occasion fawn a little too much on their potential paymasters. Something like this must have happened to Drayton on the accession of James I in 1603 when he hurriedly published "To the Majesty of King James, A Gratulatory Poem". His compliments were received with indifference by the monarch, and one contemporary hinted that he had been too hasty in paying his addresses to the new sovereign –

> "Think 'twas a fault to have the verses seen
> Praising the King ere they had mourned the Queen."

Elizabethan and Jacobean writers gloried in England's newly found patriotism: Shakespeare exalted our history in his plays, Drayton in his poetry. There was his "Legend of Piers Gaveston", the favourite of Edward II executed by rebellious earls on Blacklow Hill outside Warwick. There was "The Barons' Wars" or "Mortimeriados", the sequel in that unhappy reign. And there was the magnificent "Ballad of Agincourt", inspired, it is believed, by a rough ballad he heard a minstrel sing:

> "Fair stood the wind for France,
> When we our sails advance,
> Nor now to prove our chance,
> Longer will tarry."

Drayton's most notable work, however, was the mammoth "Polyolbion" (from the Greek meaning 'having many blessings') which he wrote between 1598 and 1622 and the first part of which he published in 1613. In this epic work of some 30,000 lines divided into some thirty 'songs' he endeavoured to awaken the interest of his readers in the beauties of their country. It is an amalgam of topography and history, based on the works of the antiquarians Leland and Camden, in which he aimed at giving "a chorographical description of all the tracts, rivers, mountains, forests and other parts of Great Britain." We see in his opening picture –

> "The sundry varying soils, the pleasures infinite,
> Where heat kills not the cold, nor cold expels the heat,
> The calms too mildly small, nor winds too roughly great,
> Nor night doth hinder day, nor night the day doth wrong,
> The summer not too short, the winter not too long."

Those 30,000 lines were, however, probably far too long for contemporaries who preferred a verse form of only fourteen lines, and his name subsequently seems to have passed into oblivion until his poetry was rediscovered in the nineteenth century. Even in his own day he was not a 'popular' poet. Judging by his frequent alterations to the poems, he was often dissatisfied with his own verse, and judging also by the equally frequent alterations to titles and collections, he had his difficulties with the printers! Nevertheless, he may well have been the rival poet alluded to in the sonnets of Shakespeare – despite the fact that they are believed to have been personal friends! Moreover, the quality of his poetry was such that in 1626 he was referred to as Poet Laureate – erroneously as it happened: that title was held by another friend, Ben Jonson.

Drayton died in London in 1631 and was buried in Westminster Abbey where the epitaph on the monument erected to him by the Countess of Dorset was probably composed by Jonson:

> "Do, pious marble, let thy readers know,
> What they, and what their children owe,
> To Drayton's name; whose sacred dust
> We recommend unto thy trust;
> Protect his memory, and preserve his story,
> Remain a lasting monument of his glory..."

Anne and Henry Rainsford had made their home in the manor house of Clifford Chambers, near Stratford, and Drayton had often stayed there. He described it in the "Polyolbion":

> "Dear Clifford's seat, the place of health and sport
> Which many a time hath been the Muse's quiet port."

It would have been at Clifford Chambers that Dr. John Hall, Shakespeare's son-in-law, attended him. The doctor wrote in his case-book, "Mr. Drayton, an excellent poet, labouring of a tertian (a fever) was cured by an emetic infusion of syrup of violets." Drayton wrote an elegy to Rainsford when he died in 1621, "Upon the Death of His Incomparable Friend, Past all Degrees that was so dear to me", and he continued to visit the widowed matron, the Muse of his younger days, until a few months before his death. He died a bachelor, his love unrequited, and so –

> "Since there's no help, come let us kiss and part:
> Nay, I have done; you get no more of me,
> And I am glad, yea, glad with all my heart,
> That thus so cleanly I myself can free;
> Shake hands for ever, cancel all our vows,
> And when we meet at any time again,
> Be it not seen in either of our brows,
> That we one jot of former love retain.

Now at the last gasp of love's latest breath,
When, his pulse failing, passion speechless lies,
When faith is kneeling by his bed of death,
And innocence is closing up his eyes,
Now, if thou wouldst, when all have given him over,
From death to life thou mightst him yet recover."

— 10 —

Warwickshire's First Local Historian

S IR William Dugdale, born at Shustoke, near Coleshill, in 1605, can be regarded as one of the first English historians of modern times as distinct from the chroniclers of the Middle Ages, and his concern for meticulous detail has preserved for us many records of olden times, whether of fact or legend, which might otherwise have been lost for ever. Owing much to his older Warwickshire contemporary Sir Simon Archer, Dugdale was destined for work of an antiquarian and heraldic nature. He was to become successively Blanch Lyon Pursuivant, Rouge Croix Pursuivant, Chester Herald, Norroy King of Arms and, finally, Garter King of Arms, and on reaching that summit of his profession in the Heralds' Office in 1667 he was knighted.

Though not active in the Royalist army, Dugdale's work in those times of upheaval was of considerable importance to the establishment. Fearing depredations by the Puritans, he had drawings made of the monuments and copies taken of the epitaphs in Westminster Abbey, St. Paul's Cathedral and a number of provincial churches. And when the Civil War broke out the more practical side of his work entailed delivering royal warrants demanding the submission of garrisons which held towns for the Parliament. As a result he was present at the Battle of Edgehill and afterwards accompanied King Charles to Oxford.

It was fortunate that his work also enabled him to pursue his hobby of historical writing. Employment in the Heralds' Office meant access to records in the Tower of London and other places, and his stay in Oxford enabled him to do considerable research in the various libraries there.

The fruit of his labours was the publication in 1656 of his magnum opus, "The Antiquities of Warwickshire", a work we are now more familiar with in the expanded two-volume second edition of 1730. The county is described hundred by hundred, and the bulk of the work consists of histories of county families and religious foundations and their properties. Though legend is not always distinguished from historical fact, it is remarkable for general accuracy and the scrupulous citing of authorities.

Dugdale's other great work was his three-volume "Monasticum Anglicorum" completed in 1673. This was a time of Catholic scares – the heir to the throne, the future James II, was a Catholic – and what was meant to be a purely scholarly work produced an outcry because its details listing property taken from Catholics during Reformation times was seen by Protestants as a help to them to claim its recovery if ever their cause triumphed!

Other works by Dugdale include the publication of official "Visitations" he made to several counties as a herald; a book on "The Baronage of England"; and in 1658 "The History of St. Paul's Cathedral". This last was timely for the descriptions and drawings of a building which was to be destroyed in the Great Fire of London only eight years later.

Dugdale bequeathed many of his manuscripts to the Ashmolean Museum in Oxford, founded by his son-in-law Elias Ashmole, and they are now in the Bodleian Library.

Our Warwickshire antiquarian had bought Blythe Hall, near Coleshill, as a young man, and it was there that he died in 1686.

— 11 —

Nonconformist Divine

LTHOUGH not as well known as John Bunyan or Richard Baxter, Samuel Annesley was one of the leading Puritans of the seventeenth century. He was born at Haseley, north-west of Warwick, in 1620 and baptised in the little church there: the fifteenth century font is still in use. He was educated at the Free School (presumably Henry VIII School) in Coventry, and at Queen's College, Oxford. He was destined for holy orders from an early age – like others at the time he seems to have been both episcopally and presbyterially ordained – and he soon commenced a practice which he continued all his life of reading twenty chapters of the Bible a day.

His first post in 1644 was as chaplain on board the "Globe" to Robert Rich, Earl of Warwick, the Lord High Admiral of the Parliamentary fleet, and he was to have a second spell at sea a few years later. Back on land, he was presented to the living of Cliffe in Kent, was awarded the degree of

Haseley Church.

Doctor of Civil Law by the University of Oxford, and preached a sermon in July 1648 before the House of Commons in which he advocated that they gave up negotiating with a deceitful king.

In 1657 he was nominated by Oliver Cromwell to be Lecturer at St. Paul's and the following year was presented by Richard Cromwell to the vicarage of St. Giles, Cripplegate. But, of course, at the Restoration not only was the monarchy restored but also the episcopal Anglican Church. Following the passing of the Act of Uniformity in 1662, 2000 Nonconformist ministers were expelled from their livings in the Great Ejectment on St. Bartholomew's Day (August 24th) that year. Samuel Annesley was offered promotion if he would conform – the authorities obviously knew his worth – but he went like all the rest, refusing to subscribe to episcopacy and the Thirty-Nine Articles or to give his "unfeigned consent and assent" to everything in the Prayer Book.

Thereafter, through some twenty-five years or so of persecution he preached privately whenever opportunity offered, though he had his goods confiscated for keeping an unauthorised conventicle. Fortunately, he lived to see the Glorious Revolution and the toleration of Dissent, and he died on December 31st 1696.

Dr. Annesley married twice and had twenty-five children! Susanna, the youngest of them all who was to become the mother of John Wesley, became an Anglican at her own wish as a teenager, and it says much for their tolerance and understanding in an intolerant age that this did not destroy the love between father and daughter. Incidentally, it is said that Samuel Annesley was never quite sure whether he had two dozen children or a quarter of a century!

— 12 —

Cathedral Architect

AS you travel north on the M40 from Warwick to Birmingham, a strange obelisk comes temporarily into view on the right. Bearing no inscription, it was raised by the first Baron Archer of Umberslade in 1749. Suggested reasons for its erection by this loyal Whig range from thanks for his peerage to thanks for the defeat of Bonnie Prince Charlie. This Lord Archer was the grandson of Thomas Archer, the M.P. for Warwick in the time of Charles II, and the great-grandson of Sir Simon Archer, the antiquary. But more importantly he was the nephew of the subject of this Ripple, Thomas Archer, the architect, who died in 1743 and was a pupil of Vanbrugh and a contemporary of Smith of Warwick. He lived in Jury Street in Warwick in the building much altered which is now the Lord Leycester Hotel. When the Great Fire of Warwick spread along the north side of the street on that September day in 1694, it mercifully stopped just short of his residence.

Thomas Archer held honorary office as Groom Porter to Queen Anne and the first two Georges, but it is as an architect that he gained fame. He designed St. John's Church, Smith Square, Westminster; Heythorpe Hall in Oxfordshire; Wrest Park House in Bedfordshire; Chettle House in Dorset; and probably the family's new Umberslade Hall. But his most famous building was St. Philip's Church in Birmingham, which later became the Anglican cathedral.

Another of his buildings has recently had a profound effect upon someone currently serving a prison sentence. On the run, escaping from prison after robbing banks and building societies, Peter Wayne sheltered in St. Paul's Church, Deptford one stormy night and was so struck by its architecture that he underwent a conversion and is now researching Thomas Archer in depth with a view to publication, having been allowed out on licence to visit Archer's other buildings.

— 13 —

The Spectator

JOSEPH Addison was an all-rounder – essayist, poet and statesman, friend of Swift, Latin scholar and Whig pamphleteer. He was born in 1672, the son of Rev. Lancelot Addison of Milston, near Amesbury in Wiltshire, and educated at Charterhouse and Queen's and Magdalen Colleges, Oxford. He was M.P. for Lostwithiel in Cornwall from 1708 to 1709 and for Malmesbury from 1709 until his death in 1719, though he never once spoke in the House of Commons! He was more effective for his party as a writer of pamphlets. Twice Secretary to the Lord Lieutenant of Ireland, he was appointed Secretary of State in 1717 but had to resign his position the following year because of ill-health. Contributing at first to Sir Richard Steele's "The Tatler", he followed this with 555 daily issues of "The Spectator" during 1711 and 1712 jointly with Steele. Addison wrote 274 of the issues, perfecting the essay as a literary form and distinguishing each article by a signature of one of the letters in the word CLIO, the muse of

Bilton Hall.

history. In these essays, purportedly edited by members of the fictional Spectator Club, Mr. Spectator provides a picture of the social life of the time. Steele invented another club member, Sir Roger de Coverley, but it was Addison who developed this portrait of a perfect English country gentleman whose great-grandfather was supposed to have invented the dance of that name. Addison also wrote a play "Cato", an opera "Fair Rosamund", a poem "The Campaign" celebrating the victory of Blenheim, and a few hymns including "The Spacious Firmament on high" and "When all Thy mercies, O my God, My rising soul surveys". But it was as an essayist that he was supreme.

And the Warwickshire connection? In 1711 Addison bought the estate of Bilton, near Rugby, from the Boughton family for £10,000. This included Jacobean Bilton Hall which has now been converted into flats. In 1716 at the age of forty-four he married Charlotte, Countess of Warwick, the widow of Edward Rich, Earl of Warwick. Alas, their life together at Bilton was all too short. Addison died three years later, leaving his wife an only daughter Charlotte who never married, and he was buried in Poet's Corner in Westminster Abbey.

— 14 —

Shell Work and Paper Craft

MRS. Delany was famous as a lady of letters in the fashionable London life of the second half of the eighteenth century, and the six volumes of her posthumously published "Autobiography and Correspondence" give a spirited account of the court and society life of the day. She was a great friend of King George III, Queen Charlotte and other members of the royal family, the King actually giving the old lady a house at Windsor in 1785. She was also a member of the Blue Stocking Circle, an informal group of intelligent, learned and sociable men and women which also included Hannah More, Horace Walpole, Samuel Johnson and Joshua Reynolds among its members. The origin of the name almost certainly lies with the stockings of Benjamin Stillingfleet, who was too poor to possess fine evening clothes and came to the circle's receptions in his blue worsted stockings.

As a lady of leisure Mrs. Delany had two great hobbies. One she began when she was over seventy. Her intricate flower work in paper mosaics, of which she produced nearly a thousand in the ten years between 1774 and 1784, have recently been retrieved from oblivion by Ruth Hayden. But it is her other hobby of shell work which is of greater interest to us in Warwickshire. For Mrs. Delany often stayed with her younger sister, Anne Dewes, the mistress of Wellesbourne Hall. Besides decorating two fireplaces there with shells, her handiwork still exists today at Walton. There is an eighteenth century summer house in the grounds of Walton Hall, variously described as a hunting lodge or the Bath Room because of the icy waters of the grotto beneath. This octagon room boasts a shell work ceiling designed by Mrs. Delany, which continues to be preserved in excellent condition.

Mrs. Delany died in 1788 at the age of 88. History remembers her as old Mrs. Delany, without benefit of Christian name. Yet like all of us she was young once.

She was born Mary Granville on May 14th 1700, at Coulston in Wiltshire, the daughter of Bernard Granville, the younger brother of Lord Lansdowne. She was descended from an old Cornish family and, despite the difference in spelling, was related both to Sir Richard Grenville of the "Revenge" who fought "one against fifty-three" at Flores in the Azores, and to Sir Bevil

The ceiling of the Bath House at Walton.

Grenville who died fighting for his king in the Civil War on Lansdowne hill outside Bath. In her teens Mary lived in the village of Buckland, just over the Gloucestershire border, so she almost qualifies as a "Ripple" here too. At Buckland she was admired by a young man named Twyford. But unfortunately she was sent to stay with her uncle Lord Lansdowne at Longleat, and there she met Alexander Pendarves of Roscrow, near Falmouth, who was nearly sixty, fat, sulky and engaged in a desperate quarrel with a nephew. He wished to marry Miss Granville, probably to spite his nephew. Lord Lansdowne approved of the match, as did her penniless father, Pendarves having a fine estate, and he told his niece that he would have her lover Twyford dragged through a horse-pond should he venture to appear. The seventeen-year-old Mary Granville yielded, and married Pendarves in February 1718. One morning seven years later she awoke to find her husband dead in bed beside her, having mistaken the death rattle for his usual drunken snoring.

As a young widow she returned to Buckland, and it was here that she met a young Oxford don named John Wesley through their mutual friends the Kirkhams who lived in the neighbouring village of Stanton. They corresponded for a while, adopting classical noms-de-plume as was the fashion of the time: he wrote as Cyrus, she as Aspasia. The correspondence petered out when Mary Pendarves went to Ireland where she was to enjoy the friendship of Jonathan Swift and his circle. She remarried in June 1743 when one of these Irish friends, Dr. Patrick Delany, Dean of Down, came over to England expressly to propose to her. It was a happy though childless marriage, but Dr. Delany's death in 1768 left her a widow again for the last twenty years of her life, and it is as old Mrs. Delany that posterity remembers her.

— 15 —

Amazing Grace

"Amazing grace (how sweet the sound)
That saved a wretch like me!
I once was lost, but now am found,
Was blind, but now I see."

This hymn which was 'top of the pops' some years ago, was written by the 'wretch' John Newton, a slave-trader who became an evangelical clergyman and famous hymn writer.

Born in London in 1725, he was the son of a captain in the merchant service engaged in the Mediterranean trade. His mother gave him some early religious training, but she died when he was only seven years of age, and his father remarried. He went to sea with his father at the age of eleven and made half a dozen voyages with him in the next few years before his father retired from the service in 1742. John continued at sea, and after returning from a voyage to Venice, was press-ganged on board H.M.S. Harwich in February 1744. Conditions in the navy were far worse even than the terrible privations of the merchant service, and although he was made a midshipman through his father's influence, he soon deserted. When he was recaptured he was flogged with the cat-o'-nine-tails and degraded to the rank of ordinary seaman. At his own request he was then transferred off Madeira on to a slave trading ship which took him to the coast of Sierra Leone.

During all these wanderings and tribulations Newton had lost all sense of religion. He became a servant – almost a slave himself – to a brutal slave trader on the Guinea coast. Fortunately, after a while he was able to transfer to the employ of a more reasonable man who soon realised that his new assistant was reliable despite the blasphemous tongue which shocked him as a respectable slave dealer! Then early in 1747 Newton was rescued from the West African coast by a ship's captain who had been asked by his father to look out for him. However, this was not the end of his troubles: this ship the "Greyhound" did not return to England for another year, and when it did it was badly damaged in a severe storm. The deliverance from this storm suddenly awakened in him a belief in a merciful God, and to the end of his days he kept the anniversary of this 'conversion' (March 10th 1748) as a day of humiliation and thanksgiving for his 'great deliverance'.

Yet, incomprehensibly to us, for the next few years Newton was to be a slave trader. First he made the triangular voyage to West Africa, the West Indies and back as mate in the "Brownlow", then as captain of the "Duke of Argyle" and finally on two more voyages as captain of "The African". True, he treated the slaves reasonably well on the voyage across the Atlantic, but then if they fell ill or died the profits were less! True also, of course, in later life he repented of this mental block which saw his fellow human beings as so much cattle, and he became a staunch abolitionist, but at the time he did not question the morality of the slave trade, and "Amazing Grace" was actually composed when he was in command of a slaver! Indeed he only gave up the sea and slave trading in 1754 owing to ill-health – to take the post of surveyor of the tides at Liverpool for five years (1755 – 60).

At this time Newton, eagerly pursuing self-taught studies, was greatly influenced by Whitefield and Wesley. He soon resolved to undertake some ministerial work, but he was undecided whether to become a Church of England clergyman or a Dissenting minister. In December 1758 he applied for holy orders but was turned down. It was at this time whilst he was unsure of his future course that he served for a short while (probably for three months) in 1760 as supply pastor at the Independent chapel newly erected in Cow Lane (Brook Street), Warwick.

In the latter half of the previous (seventeenth) century, a Mr. Vennor was constable in Warwick. On a certain Sunday it was his duty, with other officers, to break up a meeting of Nonconformists and take them into custody under the Conventicle Act. They took their prisoners to the Court House and waited for the magistrates to come out of Church. When the magistrates did not arrive, Vennor, a humane man, induced his fellow constables to agree that each of them should take a prisoner home to dinner. Vennor's prisoner proved so interesting and persuasive in conversation that the constable himself afterwards became a Nonconformist. His grandson in turn was a Nonconformist, and it was through an invitation from this grandson that Newton came to minister in Warwick.

Newton retained pleasant memories of Warwick. Afterwards at Olney he was heard to say "that the very name of Warwick would make his heart leap for joy." Years later in writing to a friend he commented, "In returning from Shropshire, we spent two nights at Warwick, the first time I have been there since....There likewise we enjoyed and sorrowed. The people among whom my mouth was first opened, and where I found some sweet encouragement in my entrance on the ministry, will always be dear to me; they are at present but few, but those few are lively and steady." Indeed Vennor continued to be Newton's lifelong friend and correspondent. On July 19th 1782 Newton wrote to him, "How many mercies has the Lord bestowed upon me since my first visit to Warwick, which is now more than twenty-two years! I often think of that time with pleasure. There the Lord opened my mouth. Many retired places in your neighbourhood were endeared to me by seasons which I can still remember, when I was enabled to seek the Lord, and to pour out before Him prayers which He has since abundantly answered."

He secured ordination at last in 1764 through the good offices of the evangelical Earl of Dartmouth who then appointed him curate at Olney in the north of Buckinghamshire. As the vicar was non-resident, Newton was the actual pastor and for fifteen years he ministered most effectively to the poor people employed in the lace industry there. They rallied round him to such an extent that a gallery had to be added to the church to accommodate the increased congregations. His stay at Olney, however, is most notable for his close friendship with the poet William Cowper and for their publication in 1779 of the famous "Olney Hymns". 280 of these were Newton's. In addition to "Amazing Grace" there were included the equally well-known

"How sweet the name of Jesus sounds,
In a believer's ear!
It soothes his sorrows, heals his wounds,
And drives away his fear."

and others such as

"Glorious things of Thee are spoken
Zion, city of our God."

and

"One there is above all others
Well deserves the name of friend."

(Cowper contributed a further 68 including "God moves in a mysterious way His wonders to perform").

In January 1780 Newton became vicar of St. Mary Woolnoth in the City of London where he remained until his death at the age of 82 in 1807. It was only the second evangelical appointment in the capital – and the church was crowded.

It was the ex-slave trader who spurred on the greatest of the abolitionists. William Wilberforce, a young M.P. given up to pleasurable pursuits, wrote to ask Newton for a secret meeting for "some serious conversation" – secret because it was regarded as disreputable for one of his social standing to turn to one of those evangelical preachers! Wilberforce records in his diary: "Called upon Old Newton – was much affected in conversing with him....when I came away I found my mind in a calm, tranquil state, more humbled, and looking more devoutly up to God." Newton in fact persuaded Wilberforce not to take holy orders, but to remain in politics and fight the slave trade from there. Wilberforce said he never spent half an hour in Newton's company without hearing some allusion to slavery and to his remorse for his early involvement in the trade. And in 1788 Newton helped Wilberforce by publishing a long confessional pamphlet, "Thoughts upon the African Slave Trade", a temperate, restrained but ghastly recital of the facts from his own experience.

A year before his death a friend suggested that Newton should give up preaching. The old man replied, "What! Shall the old African blasphemer stop while he can still speak?" Appropriately for an old navy man the last service at which he preached was a special service to raise money for the sufferers of the Battle of Trafalgar.

Retaining his humour to the end, he said to one friend, "I am packed and sealed and waiting for the post." To another he commented, "I am like a person going a journey in a stage-coach, who expects its arrival every hour, and is frequently looking out of the window for it." The coach came on December 21st 1807, and it had been sufficiently delayed for Newton to learn that the Act abolishing the slave trade, against which he had campaigned since his Warwick days, had at last become law.

— 16 —

Revolt against Revolution

AN obscure revolt against the French Revolution is of interest to us because the high point of rebel success was the capture of Warwick's twin town of Saumur with its fairy-tale castle. This revolt occurred in 1793 in the wine-growing area of Western France south of the Loire in what was known as the *Vendée Militaire,* an area much larger than the present *départment* of that name. It was a spontaneous rising of the people, or rather a series of such risings, against injustice perpetrated by those in Paris who had themselves thrown off the shackles of oppression but were prepared to be just as oppressive themselves.

This Vendean uprising was only incidentally concerned with the restoration of the monarchy which the Republic had overthrown: it was essentially a crusade, a war of religion, in defence of the Roman Catholic faith. In 1791 the Civil Constitution of the Clergy required all priests, who were to be elected and salaried like civil servants, to take an oath of allegiance to the state. In parts of the Vendée 90 per cent refused, becoming 'nonjuring' or 'refractory', and were replaced by 'constitutional' priests whose offices were regarded as valueless by the local people, especially as these priests were banned by the Pope.

The matter was exacerbated in 1793 by the *'Levée en Masse',* selective conscription, with each village required to supply a quota of men for the armies of Revolutionary France. The peasants were unwilling to fight for ideals they deplored, scuffles grew into riots beginning in the town of St. Florent, and riots into war. A series of individual spontaneous revolts eventually coalesced, and the local gentry (who hereabouts, unlike elsewhere in France, were benevolent and well-liked) were reluctantly persuaded to take the lead, nobles like the flamboyant La Rochejaquelein and the Sieur d'Elbée sharing command with the peasant Cathelineau and the former gamekeeper Stofflet.

The rising began in the March of 1793. Important provincial towns fell to the rebels – Chatillon, Cholet, Thouars, Parthenay, Fontenoy. Then in June they were emboldened to attack Saumur, a republican stronghold on the Loire outside the Vendée. Contrary to their usual ad hoc tactics they prepared their assault with considerable care, well aware that the city was protected by two rivers and an almost impregnable castle. La Rochejaquelein himself, disguised as a peasant, entered the place to reconnoitre; an unknown royalist agent spiked the guns; and for good measure their powder magazine was blown up. Shortly before mid-day on June 9th the Vendeans launched a co-ordinated attack. The fighting became particularly fierce around the castle and, surprised by the determined defence, the royalists began to waver. Fortunately a Vendean cavalry charge turned the tide, whilst retreating men drew the republican horse into a trap of devastating crossfire. By nightfall Saumur was theirs, together with 50 cannon, 1500 muskets and vast quantities of ammunition and equipment – such captures being their main source of arms supply. 300 to 400 prisoners were taken, but released once their heads had been routinely shaved!

Yet within a few days the Vendeans had evacuated the town. The peasantry were pursuing a war they could prolong, but could scarcely hope to win – they had no foreign assistance - and the part-time soldiers would go home after each campaign, abandoning conquests as soon as they were made. They were the world's first guerilla fighters, avoiding pitched battles for the most part, but picking their own terrain – foreshadowing the Boers, the Maquis and the Third World freedom fighters. Then as now the regular armies of the state found it difficult to run such will o' the wisps to ground, however untrained and inadequately armed such opponents might be.

Unfortunately the Vendean leaders could not agree among themselves and, being too far away from home, the peasant-soldiers were at a disadvantage. Repulsed before Nantes, their fate was sealed when they decided to cross the Loire and march north to Granville on the coast of Brittany for a rendezvous with a British expedition which arrived too late. As the dispirited Vendeans retraced their steps for home in the cold December weather, they were cut to pieces at Le Mans and destroyed at Savenay.

As the war had proceeded it degenerated into atrocities on both sides, but the republican revenge for the *'Grand Guerre de Vendée'* was terrible to behold. 'Infernal columns' crossed the province adopting a scorched earth policy. At Nantes the infamous *répresentant* Carrier had the rebels and their families loaded into barges and sunk in the Loire, and in the end so many corpses blocked the river that the town was in danger of a typhus epidemic.

Today there is a *Souvenir Vendean,* a society formed in the 1930s to ensure that present and future generations do not forget the tribulations of their forbears. Plaques and crosses are put up to mark the events of 1793. Many Vendeans today see little to celebrate in a revolution whose armies destroyed the region and killed 500,000 people – between a quarter and a third of the population. At Les Petits Lucs they built a chapel in memory of 563 people bayoneted as they prayed. Total war had been followed by genocide.

Saumur, outside the Vendée, escaped, but the main claim of Warwick's twin town to a place in history is as the climax of the short-lived success of this little known People's War.

— 17 —

Princess Olive

W HEN Dr. James Wilmot became Rector of Barton-on-the-Heath in the very south of the county in 1782 and brought his lively ten-year-old niece Olive to live with him, little did the folk of that remote rural parish realise that they had a potential if spurious princess in their midst. "Thou witch of wonder! " wrote the Earl of Warwick to this Olive twenty years later, "Thou Warwickshire maid! You accomplish everything you say or do!" Olive was to fulfil her regal dreams, not by the usual method of marrying a prince, but by the novel means of forging documents – and as a result for three years she was to drive her carriage openly through the streets of London as a Princess of the Blood Royal without a finger being raised to stop her.

Olive Wilmot was born in Warwick on April 3rd 1772, the daughter of Robert Wilmot, an interior decorator, and his wife Anna Maria, and baptised there twelve days later in St. Nicholas Church. Much of her early life, however, was spent at Barton with her bachelor uncle because her father had fallen into disgrace by disappearing with the rates shortly after being appointed County Treasurer!

Our whole story is one of intrigue. As a prelude, one night when Dr. Wilmot was away from home, burglars ransacked the Rectory, and the teenager Olive claimed that she had jumped out of her bedroom window at six in the morning to raise the alarm and rescue the servants who had been tied up by the robbers. Her story was accepted by the authorities, but the servants remembered that at nine the previous evening she had fired off a loaded pistol at the front door of the rectory. Could this have been a signal to the burglars lurking outside that the coast was clear?

Her father Robert was now living in London where he persuaded Dominic Serres, an artist, to get his son, John Thomas Serres, to teach Olive drawing. The young Serres, shortly to succeed his father as marine painter to the King, fell in love with his pupil, and they were married by her uncle at Barton on September 17th 1791. The marriage was to prove an unhappy one, and in 1804 they separated: she milked him of money for all she was worth, and he for his part was to have nothing to do with her subsequent claims to be a princess.

Olive tried her hand at writing, publishing among other items a memoir of her uncle – in her fertile imagination he was the author of the anonymous but scurrilous "Letters of Junius" which caused such a political scandal in their day. She also tried her hand – with more repute – at painting. Her landscapes were exhibited at the Royal Academy and in 1806 she was appointed landscape painter to the Prince of Wales.

In 1817 she made her first claim to be the daughter of the Duke of Cumberland, the brother of George III. In a petition to the King Olive alleged that she was the illegitimate daughter of the Duke and her aunt Olive Payne, sister of Dr. Wilmot and wife of a naval captain. Though Mrs. Payne was eighteen years older than the duke, circumstantial evidence seemed to support the story. The Duke of Kent (Victoria's father) believed Olive to be his cousin, and that enabled her to wheedle money out of him.

Immediately after the death of George III in 1820 Olive amplified her pretensions, now asserting that she was the legitimate daughter of the Duke of Cumberland and assuming the title of Princess Olive of Cumberland. A few days after the old king's funeral 'Princess' Olive wrote to Lord Sidmouth, the Home Secretary, setting out her claim to be the legitimate daughter of a Prince of the Blood Royal and asking for £15,000 left to her under a supposed will of George III which she had in her possession. Receiving no reply, she went a stage higher and wrote to Lord Liverpool, the Prime Minister, who courteously acknowledged the letter and referred it to the Lord Chancellor. In fact Olive never received any of this money, but it was an indication that she was as much interested in wealth as in status.

Olive also proceeded to hire a carriage, place the royal arms upon it, and drive out with her servants dressed in the royal livery. How did she get away with it? Well, it was the time of the squabble between the new King George IV and his estranged wife Caroline whom he was to refuse admittance to the Coronation. Caroline was enthusiastically received by the London crowds as a wronged Queen, and Olive was astute enough to ride on the back of that sympathy. As no action was taken to stop her, the public assumed that she too was a wronged princess. Her first public outing as a princess was to St. James's Park where she drove up to the royal entrance. Refused admittance, she sent another note to Lord Sidmouth, who, getting cold feet (his house had already been stoned by a pro-Caroline mob), sent back permission for her to enter. This she did to cheers from the crowd. She was also cheered as she drove to Drury Lane Theatre where this time she was admitted as a royal personage with no questions asked. On top of this the Lord Mayor of London invited her to the Lord Mayor's Banquet at the Guildhall where she was introduced as Princess of Cumberland and her train was held by the wives of eight aldermen. Obviously this was all part of a carefully organised publicity campaign on Olive's part.

According to her final story – elaborated and supported by what she represented as genuine documentary evidence – she was the Duke of

Cumberland's daughter not by Mrs. Payne but by Mrs. Payne's niece! She still called her mother Olive, but presumably thought that to place her in the next generation was more plausible. It was alleged that the bachelor Dr. Wilmot had secretly married back in 1749 a Princess Poniatowski, the sister of Count Stanislaus Augustus Poniatowski who later became King of Poland, and had a daughter by her, the first Olive born in 1750, who was placed in the care of Dr. Wilmot's sister Mrs. Payne. The girl won the admiration of both the Duke of Cumberland and the Earl of Warwick, but the earl gave way and the duke married her at the house of Lord Archer of Umberslade in Grosvenor Square in March 1767. The ceremony was said to have been performed by Dr. Wilmot in the presence of the Earl of Warwick and a certain Dr. James Addez, supposedly a Warwick man. A truly Warwickshire company! Of this marriage, our second 'Princess' Olive asserted that she was the child, but that ten days after her birth she was substituted for a stillborn daughter of Dr. Wilmot's brother Robert, who was thenceforth reputed to be her father!

In July 1821 'Princess' Olive was arrested for debt and moved the court for a stay in the proceedings on the grounds that as the legitimate daughter of the Duke of Cumberland she was exempt from arrest in civil cases. However, the court held that as she had already accepted bail she was too late to raise the issue of privilege. Nothing daunted, in 1823 she persuaded a gullible Member of Parliament to present a petition to the House of Commons on her behalf and move that it should be referred to a Select Committee. However, the new Home Secretary, Sir Robert Peel, declared that Mrs. Serres's contentions were baseless, and the motion was rejected without a division. As a result she spent the rest of her life in difficulties and died on November 21st 1834.

But that was not the end of the matter. Years later in 1858 one of her daughters, a Lavinia Ryves, published an "Appeal for Royalty", asserting her mother's claim and styling herself Princess Lavinia of Cumberland and Duchess of Lancaster. She proceeded to add another fictitious story based on another of her mother's forgeries: way back George III himself had secretly married a certain Hannah Lightfoot before he married Queen Charlotte. But according to this story he remarried Charlotte after Hannah's early death, leaving only the two eldest sons of his large family as illegitimate – so Olive and Lavinia never went so far as to claim the throne! Money and recognition were enough!

Finally in June 1866, 69-year-old Lavinia took advantage of the Legitimacy Declaration Act of 1861 to bring the case to court again on behalf of herself and her son – Ryves and Ryves v the Attorney-General. She petitioned the court to declare the Duke of Cumberland and her grandmother Olive Wilmot lawfully married, and thus 'Princess' Olive Serres her mother their legitimate child. All documents relating to the controversy, about seventy in all, were produced. But before the Attorney-General had finished his address for the Crown, the jury unanimously found that signatures to the key documents were forgeries and that

Lavinia had no case. Indeed even if she had won it would have been to no avail, because she would have found herself illegitimate since Olive her mother had never sought the king's permission to marry as was required of royalty under the Royal Marriages Act!

Lavinia Ryves left the court convinced that she was the victim of a cover-up, but the case proved once and for all that her mother Olive had not been a princess but an impostor. Yet as Margaret Shepard in her book "Princess Olive" writes: "Perhaps Olive is still laughing, as she did that night long ago when she fired off a pistol at the front door of Barton Rectory. If she was an impostor, then surely she should be given full honours as the most glorious impostor this country has ever known."

— 18 —

Founder of Eugenics

THE family of Sir Francis Galton, the founder of the school of eugenics, were lords of the manor of Claverdon, near Warwick. He was born in Birmingham in 1822. His mother was a Darwin, so that he was related to many of the other leading liberal intellectuals of his day.

Abandoning a proposed medical career, Galton first made his name as an explorer, notably to uncharted Damaraland, now Namibia, and as a result of his African journey he wrote a useful guide book entitled "The Art of Travel" and also played an important part on the council of the Royal Geographical Society.

Besides being elected a Fellow of the Royal Society, he was for a time secretary of the British Association for the Advancement of Science. In 1863 he published "Meteorographica, or Methods of Mapping the Weather": he had discovered anticyclones, and indeed coined the word, and can be regarded as the father of weather-forecasting.

Finally, but most importantly, spurred on by the publication of "The Origin of Species" by his cousin Charles Darwin, Galton was to take a great interest in the laws of heredity, a word also invented by him. As the tablet in the chancel of Claverdon Church states: "Many branches of Science owe much to his labours, but the dominant idea of his life's work was to measure the influence of heredity on the mental and physical attributes of mankind." His investigations into heredity extended over forty years, producing such works as "Hereditary Genius" and "Natural Inheritance". His studies were concerned with methods of improving the quality of the human race, both by better environment and by breeding from the best and restricting the offspring of the worst, though not by the means advocated later by the Nazis for a master race! For this study he coined yet another word, eugenics, and to this end he endowed a Chair of Eugenics at the University of London.

Knighted in 1909, Galton died in 1911 and was buried in the family vault on the north side of Claverdon Church.

— 19 —

Onward Christian Soldier

S ABINE Baring-Gould was the last of the squarsons, that race of squire-parsons which flourished in 18th century England but was an anachronism long before his death in his 90th year in 1924. His great-grandmother's name of Gould had been added to the family name of Baring, and he was given his grandmother's maiden name as a Christian name. Born at Exeter in 1834 to Edward and Sophia Baring-Gould, he was a pupil at Warwick School when the family lived in the town from 1845 to 1847, a time when the college was still situated in the Butts. Although he later went to Clare College, Cambridge, he received little formal education because of his parents' predilection for long periods of continental travel. Largely self-taught, he was that symbol of a bygone age, the leisured enthusiastic amateur who dabbled, often inaccurately but always entertainingly, in all manner of subjects. A polymath, he was historian and biographer, antiquary and archaeologist, guide-book writer and journalist, Anglo-Catholic propagandist and hymn-writer, and novelist and folklore and folksong recorder, all rolled into one. He was a prolific writer, fanciful yet popular (did he invent any of his stories of the saints?). Indeed it is said that in his long life he wrote far too much far too quickly. A born story-teller, his books were immensely popular in his own day, but are totally neglected now. Today we revere the accurate one-subject specialist rather than the slipshod popularising jack-of-all-trades, but nevertheless forget that we owe a debt to the type of man who gave us "Uncle Tom Cobley" and "Onward Christian Soldiers".

After seven years of teaching at Hurstpierpoint in Sussex, Baring-Gould was ordained deacon in 1864 and became curate at Horbury in Yorkshire where he threw himself into missioning and social work. Here he not only fell in love with a teenage mill girl, but flouted convention and married her. Nothing was more divisive in 19th century society than class distinction (it still is!). However here was a real life story of a King Corpetua and his beggar maid, a story the vicissitudes of which Baring-Gould recorded in his semi-autobiographical novel, "Through Flood and Flame". Caring nothing for what others thought (probably that was why he never gained preferment), Sabine sent Grace Taylor, his Eliza Doolittle, away to York for two years, there to be educated and taught the manners of polite society, paying her parents in the meantime the equivalent of her mill wages. Having been ordained priest and appointed as Vicar of the tiny parish of Dalton in Swaledale, he and Grace were married at Horbury in 1868. It proved to be a very happy marriage lasting 47 years and producing fifteen children.

With their return from a continental honeymoon began the lonely withdrawn life of a parson in the remote countryside which, with but two further changes, was to last him till the end of his days. The first change came in 1871 when he became Rector of East Mersea on the Essex salt marshes where he wrote the best of his novels, "Mehalah", a story with a strain of brutality which Swinburne compared to "Wuthering Heights".

The Gould family inheritance was a Devon estate of 3000 acres at Lewtrenchard on the north-west edge of Dartmoor in the Okehampton-Launceston-Tavistock triangle. For many years Sabine's father was the squire there and his uncle the parson. Shortly after Sabine moved to Essex his father died and he succeeded as lord of the manor. However, he continued to minister for another nine years at East Mersea until his uncle died in 1881. He then presented himself to the family living – to remain squarson of that secluded parish of a mere 300 souls for the remaining 43 years of his life. If anyone wished to find out what he was doing they had to travel to the far west and see him for themselves. Apart from his grave in the churchyard there is little to remind us of him there today, and Lewtrenchard Manor is now a country house hotel and restaurant.

Sabine Baring-Gould

Undoubtedly Baring-Gould cared greatly for his parishoners – even though he must have overawed them by announcing his pastoral visits in advance and then arriving in state in a large carriage complete with footman! – but his literary output was prodigious. He published 159 books between 1857 and 1920, each of them having been written at a standing desk! As the gentleman amateur with private means and time to spare he could pursue his writing simply because he liked it. His magnum opus was his sixteen volume "Lives of the Saints", 3600 of them, a six year task, culled in part from an older hagiography of 57 volumes! Other works of religion of his included "The Lives of the British Saints", "The Evangelical Revival", "The Origin and Development of Religious Belief" and over twenty volumes of sermons.

Then there were his hymns. In addition to "Onward Christian Soldiers", composed as a marching song for children in his Horbury days and sung to Sir Arthur Sullivan's stirring tune St. Gertrude, there have come down to us "Now the Day is Over", "Through the Night of Doubt and Sorrow", "On the Resurrection Morning" and that paraphrase of a traditional Basque Christmas carol "The Angel Gabriel from heaven came".

He wrote two volumes of "Reminiscences" and several books of travel. His "Germany" in the "Story of the Nations" series was still going around (just) when I was a boy. But as a Westcountryman it is perhaps his books on the West which arouse most interest. The most popular of his thirty novels was "In the Roar of the Sea", about Polzeath and St. Enodoc Church, more recently so beloved of John Betjeman. Sabine wrote a biography of "The Vicar of Morwenstowe", a life of the even more eccentric Robert Stephen Hawker who took a pet pig on his pastoral visitations, and left us "And Shall Trelawney Die?" and the modern harvest festival. Then there was "A Book of the West" (Devon and Cornwall), "A Book of Dartmoor", "Devonshire Characters and Strange Events" and "Cornish Characters and Strange Events". But the greatest debt which the local historian owes to Baring-Gould in this respect is the fifteen years in which he was engaged in rescuing from oblivion the folk-songs and melodies of Devon and Cornwall from the mouths of the people who sang them. Without his "Songs and Ballads of the West", "Widecombe Fair" would not have survived.

What a pity our former Warwick schoolboy never recorded any of the oral traditions of Warwickshire!

— 20 —

Socialist Pioneer

TOM Mann, one of the three leaders of the famous London dock strike of 1889, was born on April 15th 1856 in a small cottage, No.177 Grange Road, Longford, Coventry where he was to live until he was fourteen. This champion of the workers at a time when trade unions were still weak, was the son of Thomas Mann, a clerk at Victoria Colliery, Bell Green. His mother died when he was only two, and he had only three years' education at schools at Foleshill and Little Heath. At the age of nine, like Joseph Arch, he became a bird scarer – on the colliery farm, and he was only ten when he went down the pit. He had to crawl on his hands and knees, stripped to the waist, along passages only three feet high and three feet wide, dragging a sledge loaded with dirt or coal by a thong fastened round his waist. After two years of this, he was allowed to work on the pit bank and this he did until he was fourteen, from six in the morning to six at night.

The colliery was closed after a series of fires and his father got work in Birmingham. Here, after a short spell as a printer's devil, the teenager was apprenticed for seven years as a turner in an engineering works – on a sixty hour week plus unpaid overtime: he had to carry on until eight in the evening.

This question of working hours drew his attention to trade unionism. A five month unofficial strike in 1872 succeeded in getting the working day reduced to nine hours, but no thanks to the official union. Should not the trade unions fight, reasoned Mann, instead of weakly trying to negotiate?

As it was, because of the success of the strike, however achieved, his work now finished at the early hour of five o'clock. He put his newly-found spare time to good effect by catching up on the education he had missed: he attended classes three evenings a week and, like so many self-educated men of his day, made good use of the public library.

He moved to London in 1877 after completing his apprenticeship, but because of the economic situation it was three years before he found regular employment at his trade as a turner. He was soon branded as an agitator. He founded an Eight Hours League in Battersea where men were working twelve hours a day and more in an area of mass unemployment. In a pamphlet which he published in 1886 entitled "What a Compulsory

Eight Hour Day Means", he pointed out the obvious that such a day would indeed reduce unemployment. The notoriety he gained prevented him from keeping regular employment. Disillusioned by trade unionism he was appointed as a permanent organiser by the radical Social Democratic Federation and spent the next two years covering Tyneside and Lancashire on their behalf.

But in 1889 Tom Mann returned to London for his finest hour – the organisation of the London Dock Strike with Ben Tillett and John Burns. This was a protest against the spasmodic and terrible working conditions then existing. The strike involved fifty miles of docks and 15,000 pickets. Tom was in the thick of it, averaging an eighteen to twenty hour day for five weeks. The strike ended in victory for the dockers: sixpence an hour and eightpence for overtime plus a new system of work. In gratitude the Dockers' Union elected Tom their president, a position he held until 1893.

Whither now for our restless spirit? He was to serve on the Royal Commission on Labour alongside Sidney Webb from 1891 to 1894. He decided after a short membership that the Fabian Society was too middle-class and gradual for him; he continued to be dissatisfied with the ineffectiveness of the older trade unions; and he turned down the post of secretary to the Labour Department set up by the President of the Board of Trade on the ground that he would rather be with the workers outside, rousing them to make full use of the new department. It appears he was even offered ordination, but declined: he didn't see that he could effectively work for the reform of working conditions through the Church of England!

Tom Mann's birthplace, Longford, Coventry.

Instead, in February 1894, he became secretary of the Independent Labour Party, and unsuccessfully contested parliamentary elections on its behalf in Colne Valley, North Aberdeen and Halifax. After three years he resigned this post because of the demands on his time of another organisation he had just helped to found – the International Transport Workers' Federation which agitated among dock workers in France, Spain and the Low Countries. Then in 1898 he founded the first union for unskilled labourers, the Workers' Union, of which he became general secretary.

In the first decade of the new century, however, Britain heard little of him. Not that he was idle! At the end of 1901 he left for New Zealand. He moved on to Australia the following year where he was to remain for eight years during which time he was twice arrested for his agitation. Finally he returned to London via a visit to South Africa after an absence of nine years.

In 1911 he was at the centre of strikes throughout the ports of Britain organised by the Seamen's and Dockers' Unions which led to conditions at the docks being further improved – though not before the Riot Act had been read in Liverpool, the military called in and two dockers killed when the troops opened fire. One result was a "Don't Shoot" appeal to soldiers, a pamphlet off-printed from the periodical "The Syndicalist" with which Tom Mann was associated as chairman of the International Syndicalist League. Not only were the printer and editor sent to prison, but when Mann read the appeal at several meetings during the first national miners' strike in 1912, he was arrested on a charge of inciting to mutiny. In court he argued that a soldier when engaged in assisting the civil authority was a citizen and should be treated as such. He got six months, but he was released after only seven weeks as a result of parliamentary and public pressure.

Next he became the general secretary of the Amalgamated Engineering Union from 1919 to 1921. In 1916 he had joined the British Socialist Party which became the nucleus of the British Communist Party of which he was a founder-member in 1920. In 1921 he attended the first Congress of the Red International of Labour Unions in Moscow, and in 1924 unsuccessfully stood as a Communist for the East Nottingham constituency. From then until 1932 he was chairman of the National Minority Movement which, under Communist direction, sought to use trade union organisation to achieve workers' control of industry. And he extended his agitation abroad – at various times he was deported from Holland, Germany and Canada.

In December 1932 he was sentenced to two months imprisonment on refusing to be bound over to keep the peace after agitating among the unemployed in London, but when he was charged in 1934 at Glamorgan Assizes, along with Harry Pollitt, with uttering seditious speeches, he was acquitted. As late as 1938 when he was 78 years of age he went to Stockholm to assist the Swedish Communist Party in its municipal campaigns. He died at Grassington, Yorkshire, on March 13th 1941, a month short of his 85th birthday.

This tireless champion of the underdog returned to his native Coventry a few times in his later years to lead May Day rallies. There is a Tom Mann Club at Stoke Green and a Tom Mann old people's home appropriately sited at Longford.

His birthplace there still stands, and the plaque affixed to the cottage reads: "1856 – 1956. This plaque was erected by the Executive Council of the Amalgamated Engineering Union to commemorate the 100th anniversary of the birth on this site on 15th April 1856 of Tom Mann who was the first general secretary of the Amalgamated Engineering Union and who devoted the whole of his life to the service of the Trade Union and Labour movement and the working class throughout the world."

— 21 —

The Handsomest Young Man in England

"Stands the church clock at ten to three?
And is there honey still for tea?"

Well, Mary Archer, Jeffrey's wife (they are the present occupants of Grantchester's Old Vicarage), does indeed sell 'Ten to Three' honey for charity. But the church clock doesn't stand at ten to three and never did so in Rupert Brooke's day: it was stuck at a quarter to eight. However his war sonnets, rapidly followed by his death in 1915, made him and the village so famous that the hands were then sentimentally moved to ten to three until the village raised enough cash to mend them in the 1920s. They were again moved to that time when the clock stopped a second time in 1992, and Seiko, the Japanese watch company, stepped in with £1,000 towards the repair.

Grantchester's attitude to Rupert Brooke is somewhat ambivalent. The excellent illustrated guide book to the village mentions him with approval and contains several quotations from his poems. But the business about the clock is still said to rankle among Grantchester's old stagers, as does the change of name of the local hostelry from the Rose and Crown to the Rupert Brooke. His name appears among the seventeen dead on the village's 1914 – 18 roll of honour on the war memorial. But to some local people he was a Cambridge University yuppy who didn't live in the village for very long, and a war poet who died without having heard a shot fired in anger.

However, in any case, Rugby has more claim to Rupert Brooke than Grantchester. He was born on August 3rd 1887 at No.5 Hillmorton Road, a small villa near Rugby School where his father William Parker Brooke was a master. When the boy was five years old his father became a housemaster and the family moved into the school to a house called School Field, and after prep. school at nearby Hillbrow, Rupert himself entered Rugby School in 1901 and was put in his father's house. Though he had phases of deep depression and deliberately cultivated eccentricities,

53

he was happy and popular at school. He became head of house and from an early age had a great love of literature. But also won school colours at both rugby and cricket. His was a balanced combination of the athletic and the intellectual: as Edward Marsh described him, "always with a ball in his hand and a book in his pocket". And he was uncommonly handsome.

A classical scholarship took him to King's College, Cambridge from 1906 to 1909. He took a room at The Orchard, Grantchester. But in the New Year of 1910 his father became seriously ill and he was called to take temporary charge of School Field. His father died and Rupert stayed on as acting housemaster till the end of term when his mother moved out of

Rupert Brooke's statue, Rugby.

school and made her home at No.24 Bilton Road where he became a frequent visitor. Back in Cambridge he decided to work for a fellowship (which he obtained at King's in March 1913) and he moved from The Orchard to The Old Vicarage next door. This was to become the title of the poem written in Berlin in 1912 which concludes with the famous couplet about the clock:

"Just now the lilac is in bloom,
All before my little room;
And in my flower beds, I think,
Smile the carnation and the pink,
And down the borders, well I know,
The poppy and the pansy blow."

In his early twenties Rupert Brooke had an unhappy love affair with a Katherine Cox which caused a serious breakdown in his health. He was later to fall in love with a Cathleen Nesbitt whom he would possibly have married had he lived. But at this time one gets the impression of a mixed-up young man drifting rather aimlessly. When he recovered from the nervous breakdown he entered a new phase of his life, spending more time in London, mixing with society, theatrical and literary people. He came to have a wide circle of friends in high places: Henry James, Hugh Dalton, Gwen Raverat, Geoffrey Keynes (the brother of the economist), Edward Marsh (parliamentary private secretary to Winston Churchill as First Lord of the Admiralty and later Brooke's biographer) and Violet Asquith (Bonham-Carter). As a result of the last named friendship he dined more than once at No.10 Downing Street. Rupert was involved in the "Poetry Review" and in the planning of the book "Georgian Poetry". In 1913 the "Westminster Gazette" commissioned him to write a series of travel features for them, and so he set out on a year of travels via Canada, the United States, Hawaii, Fiji, New Zealand and Tahiti.

When war broke out in 1914 Rupert Brooke volunteered. With Marsh's assistance he and his friend Denis Browne obtained commissions as sub-lieutenants in the R.N.V.R. to serve in the Royal Naval Division. In October 1914 they sailed to Antwerp to relieve the Belgians, but they arrived too late and after moving into trenches withdrew without seeing any action. His five "War Sonnets" were finished on his last leave at No.24 Bilton Road at the end of that December. In the February his Hood battalion, which included Browne, Bernard Freyberg and the Prime Minister's son Arthur Asquith, sailed for the Dardanelles. The battalion trained in Egypt. Rupert fell ill with dysentery at Port Said but refused an offer of convalescence ashore or a staff job and sailed instead as intended with the "Grantully Castle". The next anchorage was the Greek island of Skyros. Here he went ashore and took part in a field day, but back on board it was obvious he had not fully recovered from his illness. A sore on his lip, probably an infected insect bite, became swollen and produced an abscess and blood-poisoning spread rapidly. He was transferred to the French hospital ship "Dugay-Trouin", but died the next day, April 23rd 1915.

They buried him on Skyros in a beautiful olive grove where he had rested on that field day. A simple wooden cross was inscribed in Greek: "Here lies the Servant of God, Sub-lieutenant in the English navy, who died for the deliverance of Constantinople from the Turks". Years later his mother had the cross brought home and it is now on the Brooke family burial plot in Clifton Road Cemetery in Rugby. A permanent tomb was constructed on Skyros – a bronze statue, not a likeness but a nude male figure symbolising the spirit of youth. Prior to that – in 1919 – a marble portrait medallion with "The Soldier" sonnet inscribed upon it was unveiled at Rugby School:

> "If I should die, think only this of me:
> That there's some corner of a foreign field
> That is for ever England. There shall be
> In that rich earth a richer dust concealed;
> A dust whom England bore, shaped, made aware,
> Gave, once, her flowers to love, her ways to roam;
> A body of England's, breathing English air,
> Washed by her rivers, blest by suns of home..."

Just before Rupert Brooke's death Dean Inge had read out that sonnet in an Easter Sunday sermon in St. Paul's. That was the beginning of his popular acclaim, although the fame or hype (whichever way you view it) only really began with his death. In his obituary in the "Morning Post" Lascelles Abercrombie wrote:

> "Not since Sir Philip Sidney's heroic death have we lost such a gallant and joyous type of the poet-soldier... It is well, since the Gods loved him and he died young, that he should be buried on one of the isles of Greece."

Churchill's appreciation in "The Times" was even more fulsome:

> "Rupert Brooke is dead. A telegram from the Admiralty at Lemnos tells us that this life has closed at the moment when it seemed to have reached its springtime. A voice had become audible, a note had been struck, more true, more thrilling, more able to do justice to the nobility of our youth in arms engaged in this present war, than any other – more able to express their thoughts of self-surrender, and with a power to carry comfort to those who watched them so intently from afar. The voice has been swiftly stilled. Only the echoes and the memory remain; but they will linger..."

And much more in the same vein. As one biographer writes:

"Undoubtedly the myth of the golden Apollo-like hero who died sacrificially, having given a voice to the soul of a nation at war, was very much in tune with the collective mind of those first days of the 1914 – 18 conflict."

The cruelty and horror of war were to be brought out later in the War by such poets as Wilfred Owen who wrote:

"My subject is War, and the pity of War.
The Poetry is in the pity."

Nevertheless at the time Rupert Brooke's poetry and death had a great impact on the romantic imagination of his fellow countrymen, and still does today.

— 22 —

The Most Decorated Private Soldier

JUST off the Rugby Road in Leamington, near St. Mark's Church, is a block of flats, Henry Tandey Court, named after the Leamington man who is said to have been the most decorated British private soldier in the First World War. Henry Tandey was awarded the Victoria Cross, the Distinguished Conduct Medal and the Military Medal and bar all within a six week period while serving in France in 1918 – and he was also mentioned in despatches on five occasions. He won the V.C. on September 28th that year at Marcoing near Cambrai. During a bayonet charge his platoon of Green Howards was held up by machine-gun fire. He crawled forward and located the machine-gun and knocked it out of action. He then braved a hail of bullets to rig up a plank bridge over the St. Quentin canal to enable the infantry to advance. Later the same day Tandey and eight comrades were surrounded by a number of Germans and he led a bayonet charge through them – being wounded for the third time in as many years. The citation to the V.C. read "For desperate bravery and great initiative".

Henry Tandey was born in Leamington in August 1891. He spent part of his childhood in an orphanage and before the First World War worked as a porter at the Regent Hotel in the Parade. After the War he was made a Freeman of Leamington and was one of the fifty V.C.s chosen to line the aisle of Westminster Abbey for the burial of the Unknown Soldier. He became a recruiting sergeant and when he retired from the army in 1926 he moved to Coventry where he served as a commissionaire at the old Standard motor works. Married twice, he lived first in Cope Street where Coventry Sports Centre now stands and later in the suburb of Radford. He died in December 1977 at the age of 86 and his ashes were scattered on the field in France where his bravery had won him the V.C..

Tandey's widow sold his original medals at Sotheby's in 1980 to a private collector for a record £27,000, a Leamington bid having had to stop at £1000 less. The figure was £10,000 more than the previous highest price for a group of medals which included a V.C.. However his dress medals have recently been obtained for the town and are now on display alongside his portrait in the V.C. Room of the Regent Hotel. Also in this room is a picture of Tandey carrying a wounded comrade at the Menin crossroads

The painting of Henry Tandey, V.C., carrying a wounded comrade.

after one of the early battles in October 1914. This is a copy of an original painting hanging in the officers' mess of the King's Division Depot near York.

According to legend Tandey is said to have spared the life of a certain corporal called Adolf Hitler during the Marcoing action because he was already wounded. Having been captured the injured Hitler was then returned to his own lines. Tandey could never recall coming face to face with Hitler, but when he came to power in 1933 Hitler got his staff to research British Army records to discover who his saviour was. They discovered that Tandey was the man who had led the attack on Hitler's platoon. Hitler then obtained a print of the Menin painting (he had also fought in this earlier action) and hung it in his Bavarian mountain retreat at Berchtesgaden. And when Neville Chamberlain paid his famous pre-Munich visit to Berchtesgaden in 1938, Hitler pointed out Tandey in the picture as the man who had come so near to killing him. Tandey subsequently received a telephone call from the Prime Minister passing on the Führer's best wishes. Our hero could not shoot a wounded man, but the carnage in Coventry during the Second World War made him wish in retrospect that he had done so.

As we salute Henry Tandey, Britain's Most Decorated Private Soldier of the First World War, let us remember three other Leamington men who were also awarded the V.C. in that war: Colonel John Cridlan Barrett who was born in Regent Street, Captain Arthur Kilby whose memorial is in Lillington churchyard and Corporal William Amey whose grave in Leamington cemetery bears a large carving of the Cross itself.

— 23 —

Sergeant-Major

BEFORE Lord Leatherland died in December 1992 at the age of 94 he claimed to be the oldest survivor of the First World War in regular attendance at the House of Lords.

Charles Leatherland was born at Churchover, near Rugby, in 1898, the son of an army bandsman. He lied about his age and joined up at 16. He was a gunner on the Somme and a Company Sergeant-Major in the Royal Warwickshire Regiment at 18. Many years later he ascribed his arthritic aches and pains to "being up to my arse in water on the Somme".

On demobilisation he joined the Labour Party. His first job was with Birmingham City Council, but he became a journalist, joining a local Macclesfield newspaper and rising to become assistant editor of the "Daily Herald". He was also part author of "The Book of the Labour Party" in 1925. Living in Essex, he became an Epping J.P., a member of Basildon Development Corporation, Chairman of Essex County Council and a Deputy Lieutenant for that county. He was also one of the founding fathers of the University of Essex. Surprisingly one of his recreations was fox-hunting.

Leatherland was made a life peer by Harold Wilson in 1964. One of his most joyful days in the Lords was his 90th birthday when he was entertained by top brass led by Field-Marshal Lord Carver. The field-marshal recalled that, when he was training to be an officer, the instruction in times of doubt and danger was always "Carry on, Sergeant-Major". Our Warwickshire lad who had become a sergeant-major at the tender age of 18 nodded and rocked with pleasure at the command he must have heard over seventy years before.

— 24 —

Historian Laureate

GEORGE Macaulay Trevelyan was Britain's unofficial Historian Laureate. Unfortunately he is not read so much today – his conception of history has become as unfashionable as his values but during the first half of the twentieth century he was the most famous, the most honoured, the most influential and the most widely read historian of his generation. We honour him because he was born at Welcombe, near Stratford.

The Trevelyan family originated in Cornwall. They can be traced back to Domesday and were established Cornish gentry by late mediaeval times. The family coat of arms includes a horse rising from the waves, commemorating the legendary first Trevelyan who is said to have swum his steed from St. Michael's Mount to the Cornish mainland for a wager while other knights of King Arthur's court drowned.

The historian's cadet branch of the family settled at Wallington in Northumberland, and G.M. Trevelyan established himself at nearby Hollington Hall. These Trevelyans were Indian proconsuls and the greatest historical dynasty this country has ever produced. His great-uncle was Lord Macaulay and his grandfather Sir Charles was a senior civil servant. His father Sir George Otto was a cabinet minister. They were Whigs and Liberals to the core – even though his brother Sir Charles was twice a Labour cabinet minister. G.M. Trevelyan was a member of two aristocracies: the aristocracy of birth and the aristocracy of talent. Belonging to that first aristocracy of class and privilege he never needed to earn a living: as G.M. Young put it, his work was "the fruit of leisure, of freedom, of independence". History was something his forebears had made, which his family was still making and which was thus an integral part of the fabric of his own life. As for belonging to that second aristocracy of talent and intellect, Trevelyan was related to a cousinhood of high-minded middle-class evangelical families which included Wilberforces, Darwins, Wedgwoods, Butlers, Keyneses, Stephens, Haldanes and Vaughan Williamses. He married a fellow historian Janet Penrose Ward, herself to become a Companion of Honour, who was the daughter of Mrs. Humphry Ward, the grand-daughter of Thomas Arnold, niece of Matthew Arnold and cousin of

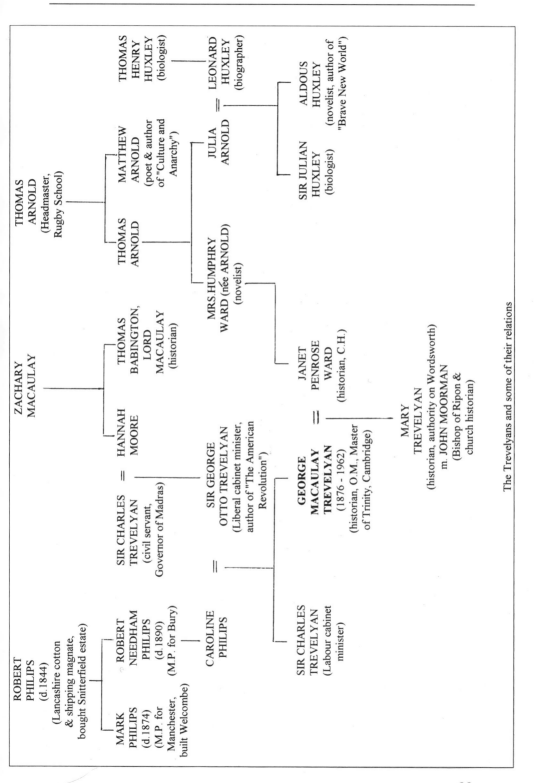

The Trevelyans and some of their relations

Julian and Aldous Huxley. It was no surprise that their daughter Mary also became an historian, an authority on Wordsworth. She married John Moorman who became Bishop of Ripon and a noted church historian.

G.M. Trevelyan was therefore at ease in the British Establishment: he took it for granted that he belonged there. But what made him an even more significant figure was that this high standing in official circles was paralleled by his unrivalled popularity with the general public as his books sold in massive numbers for more than half a century. By far his most popular work was his "English Social History" (1944) which complemented his general "History of England" (1926) and broke all records for a history book aimed at the general public. But it was not only in the narration of a wide sweep of history that he excelled. He covered particular centuries with "England under the Stuarts" (1904) in the Methuen History of England series and "British History in the Nineteenth Century" (1922) produced by his Longmans publishers. He also excelled in detailed surveys of shorter periods such as "England in the Age of Wycliffe" (1899), "Lord Grey of the Reform Bill" (1920) and trilogies on Garibaldi and the Reign of Queen Anne.

Trevelyan had been educated at Harrow and was only seventeen when he went up to Trinity College, Cambridge. After graduating with First Class Honours in the historical tripos, he held a fellowship at the college until 1903 when he left for London and independent writing. He eventually returned to Cambridge as Regius Professor of Modern History from 1927 to 1940 and Master of Trinity College from 1940 to 1951. He was Chancellor of Durham University from 1949 to 1957 and had been appointed a member of the Order of Merit as early as 1930, the highest award bestowed by the Sovereign which does not confer a title and which is open to only 24 people at any one time. Outside interests included the Chairmanship of the Estates Committee of the National Trust and the Presidency of the Youth Hostels Association. In 1945 he withdrew his name from the final short list of three for the post of Governor-General of Canada. As his biographer David Cannadine points out, he never applied for a job he did not get; indeed apart from his original fellowship at Trinity he never applied for a job at all! He died in 1962.

Through his mother Caroline Philips, Trevelyan was directly descended from one of the great Manchester mercantile dynasties whose support had been so essential to Bright and Cobden in their crusade against the Corn Laws. Our interest centres on his mother's home at Welcombe. He had homes in Northumberland and Cambridge, but he loved the Warwickshire countryside and as a boy spent every Christmas and Easter among his grandfather's Welcombe Hills. He and his brothers enjoyed playing war games with lead soldiers with their Philips grandfather.

Welcombe means "a valley with a stream". Shakespeare owned 127 acres of it in September 1614 and it remained in his family till 1669. It came into the Philips family in 1844. In 1815 Robert Philips, who had amassed a fortune in Lancashire cotton and shipping, decided to become a Warwickshire country gentleman and bought for £65,000 the Earl of Coventry's estate in Snitterfield on the northern edge of the Welcombe Hills, taking up residence in Park House, Snitterfield. A staunch teetotaller, he proceeded to close down four of the five public houses in the village. On his death in 1844 his son Mark, one of the first post-Reform Act M.P.s for Manchester, a wealthy manufacturer and great admirer of Free Trade, inherited the estate and enlarged it by acquiring Welcombe Hall, an Elizabethan manor which the previous owner had converted into a Gothic mansion. He pulled it down and then left the site empty for twenty years. Then in 1866 he decided to build the present house. It was advanced enough for him to occupy in 1870, but it was still not finished when he died in 1874. A bachelor, he was succeeded by his brother Robert Needham Philips who was no less wedded to the economy and politics of Lancashire and himself became M.P. for Bury. His daughter Caroline had married George Trevelyan in September 1869 after initial opposition to the match by both uncle and father. They had three sons, the youngest being G.M.T. born in 1876. They closed down the last remaining hostelry in Snitterfield, the Bell Brook Inn, which is now the privately owned Brook House. It was at Welcombe that Sir George wrote most of his vast work "The American Revolution" and he entertained President Theodore Roosevelt there in 1910. Caroline, who had become Lady Trevelyan when her husband inherited the baronetcy, allowed the estate tenants to buy their homes for £100, built Snitterfield village hall in 1921 and gave the land on which the Methodist chapel was built.

Somewhat surprisingly the Trevelyans sold Welcombe in 1930 to the brewer Sir Archibald Flower. He sold it again the following year to the L.M.S. Railway, and it became one of their luxury hotels, notable for the short-lived experimental 'Ro-Railer', a four-wheeled motor bus on the road and a four-wheeled railcar on the railway, which transported rail passengers direct to the door. In due course the mansion became a British Transport Hotel, but is now, along with the adjacent 18-hole golf course, owned by the Japanese. The Great Hall has become the hotel lounge; there is a Trevelyan Restaurant and a Trevelyan Bar (what would the family have said?); and you can book the Lady Caroline Suite for £500 a night!

The giant 120ft. Welcombe obelisk was erected by Robert Needham Philips in memory of his brother Mark: the eulogy on the obelisk pays tribute to Mark's work and to his "rare flow of wit and humour". His father Robert is commemorated on another face of the plinth. And after his death in 1890 the family used a third face to inscribe a testimony to Robert Needham Philips.

A stone seat beside the village war memorial on the edge of Snitterfield was dedicated by Sir George Trevelyan to the memory of his wife Caroline

The Welcombe Obelisk.

Philips. The inscription runs:- "The noble expanse visible from this spot was Shakespeare's favourite countryside. The men whose names are inscribed on the neighbouring monument gave their lives for that England which never did, and never shall, lie at the proud feet of a conqueror." No doubt their son George Macaulay Trevelyan whole-heartedly approved.

— 25 —

From Crippen to Antiquis

T HIS is the story of the greatest medical detective of all time, Sir
Bernard Spilsbury, who lived in the limelight of the criminal courts
from the Crippen trial of 1910 to the Antiquis case of 1947. Again
and again his evidence was the crucial point upon which some of the most
sensational trials of the century turned, and yet here was a reserved man
who was quite unperturbed by any other aspect of a case other than the
search for the truth.

Bernard Henry Spilsbury was born in January 1877 at No. 35 Bath Street,
Leamington, to James Spilsbury, a wholesale chemist, and his wife Marion
Joy. When he was eleven years old his father moved to London and later
to Manchester. The boy had just started at Leamington College and so
became a boarder there for a short while. He later attended University
College School, Bloomsbury, Manchester Grammar School, and Owens
College, the forerunner of Manchester University, before going up to
Magdalen College, Oxford. He went on to St. Mary's Hospital Medical
School where he was to begin the special interest in pathology which led
to a lifetime's work of 25,000 post-mortems.

He was to become Pathologist at St. Mary's, Lecturer in Morbid Anatomy
at St. Bartholomew's, and Lecturer in Forensic Medicine three times over
at University College Hospital, at the London School of Medicine for
Women, and at St. Thomas's Hospital, but it was as Pathologist to the
Home Office that he made his name, and it was the one per cent of his
autopsies in perhaps 250 murder cases which hit the headlines.

It was the trial of Dr. Crippen which first brought him before the public.
All the circumstantial evidence pointed to Crippen as the poisoner of his
wife, but it was Spilsbury's evidence of a scar from an abdominal operation
on the corpse exhumed from No. 39 Hilldrop Crescent that conclusively
proved that the body was definitely that of Mrs. Crippen.

Shortly afterwards came a second north London cause célèbre.
Frederick Henry Seddon was convicted of the murder of wealthy Eliza
Barrow. Spilsbury was able to prove that the victim did not die from natural
causes but from acute arsenical poisoning.

The case of the 'Brides in the Bath' hit the headlines even whilst the
British public was otherwise mourning the mounting casualties of the First

World War. George Joseph Smith had bigamously married three gullible women in succession, only to drown each of them subsequently in their baths in different locations. Spilsbury had the unenviable task of conducting post-mortems on the exhumed bodies of all three. Marshall Hall appeared for the defence, but Spilsbury had no difficulty in proving that neither epilepsy nor fainting fits could have caused the bodies to slump down under the water, "but if the feet at the narrow end were lifted out of the water that might allow the trunk and head to slide down the bath".

Today the little town of Hay-on-Wye on the Welsh border is famous for its bookshops. Back in April 1922 it became famous for another reason: a pillar of the local establishment was sentenced to death for murder. The domineering wife of solicitor Herbert Rowse Armstrong, who nevertheless seemed devoted to her, had died the year before, apparently of natural causes. Armstrong was a keen gardener, known to purchase quantities of arsenic for weed-killer from the local chemist. Arsenic produces symptoms so like those of natural disease that nothing would have been thought amiss had not Armstrong then attempted also to poison his rival solicitor in the town – via a contaminated buttered scone when he came to tea. The suspicions of the local G.P. who had previously not seen anything untoward in Mrs. Armstrong's death were aroused, and Armstrong was charged first with the attempted murder of his fellow solicitor, and then, after Mrs. Armstrong's body had been exhumed and examined by Spilsbury, with the murder of his wife. Because of the nature of the case Spilsbury had to carry out the post-mortem under difficult and secret conditions: once suspicions were confirmed Armstrong had to be charged in the same Hay courtroom in which he had previously sat as magistrates' clerk! At the subsequent trial at Hereford Assizes the evidence of Spilsbury and his colleagues could not be shaken: an already weakened Mrs. Armstrong had taken a large fatal dose of arsenic less than twenty-four hours before she died, and this meant that it could not have been self-administered as the defence contended. Someone else had lifted the glass to her lips – her husband.

When in June 1922 Field Marshal Sir Henry Wilson was assassinated outside his Eaton Place home by the I.R.A., Spilsbury performed the post-mortem. For his pains he had to give the I.R.A. the slip when they pursued him clutching the damning evidence in a taxi chase through central London. The following year he was knighted.

Spilsbury was also involved in the trial of Frederick Bywaters and Edith Thompson for the murder of her husband. It is now generally believed that Mrs. Thompson was wrongly executed as an accessory to the stabbing by her lover because the court was swayed by her fanciful letters. The 'hanging' judge said not a word about Spilsbury's evidence, presumably because it was as much in favour of the defence as of the prosecution. No doubt, with his rigid views on moral lapses, he disapproved of Edith Thompson's behaviour, but it is doubtful if he believed her guilty of getting rid of her husband.

Sir Bernard's masterpiece in detection, the case he himself considered was the most difficult he had ever undertaken, occurred in 1924: Patrick Mahon's murder of Emily Kaye in a holiday cottage by the Crumbles shingle of Pevensey Bay. Spilsbury had the unenviable task of piecing together the hundreds of bits of bone and flesh into which the murderer had dismembered, boiled and burnt the unfortunate girl's body.

Other famous cases in which he was involved were the Brighton Trunk Murders of the 1930s; the case of A.A. Rouse who sought to solve his amatory entanglements by attempting to fake his own death by setting his car alight with a gentleman of the road inside; and two cases of matricide. In the trial of John Donald Merrett in Edinburgh Spilsbury appeared as a defence witness, and the verdict was 'not proven'. In that of Sidney Fox at Lewes his evidence after exhumation proved that the mother had been strangled before the subsequent fire, and Fox was duly found guilty. Spilsbury also performed the autopsies after many judicial hangings, and also on a spy executed at the Tower of London during the Second World War.

Remember Alec de Antiquis, the public spirited young man, passing by on his motor bike, who tried to stop the escape of the London jewellery shop raiders, and was shot dead for his pains? It was April 1947 and Spilsbury's last murder case. Alas, his powers were fading. At the post-mortem he was sadly puzzled, looking for the exit wound of the bullet which remained in the dead man's head. It fell out during the examination. His friend Fabian of the Yard who was present handed it to him, reminding him that he had found it. But Spilsbury knew that he had not found it. Plagued by strokes and insomnia and the deaths of two of his sons, he recognised he could no longer attain his former methodical high standards and decided to end it all. Deliberately tying up his affairs as much as he could, he then took his own life in a gas-filled laboratory on the evening of December 17th 1947. The Last Post-Mortem recorded death from coronary thrombosis and carbon monoxide poisoning. A sad end for the Leamington lad who wished to die in harness searching for the truth as he knew it. On one occasion counsel had addressed him as '*St. Bernard*' – whether inadvertently in awe or deliberately in jocular tribute is disputed. Whichever it was, it was a tribute to the greatest practitioner of medical detection Britain has produced. It is good to know that Leamington has of recent years perpetuated the memory of one of its greatest sons in the name of Spilsbury Close in the north of the town.

— 26 —

Carnegie Medal Winner

VICTORIA Eleanor Doorly was a writer of children's books: "England in Her Days of Peace", "The Insect Man" (Henry Fabre), "The Microbe Man" (Louis Pasteur), "The Story of France", and "Ragamuffin King" (Henry IV of France). "The Radium Woman", which told the story of Marie Curie, was published in 1939 and won her the prestigious Library Association's Carnegie Medal for the best children's book of the year, a distinction she has enjoyed with such as Arthur Ransome and Walter de la Mare, Elizabeth Goudge and Rosemary Sutcliff, Penelope Lively and Richard Adams.

Born in 1880, of Irish descent, Eleanor Doorly was the daughter of Capt. Anton Doorly. Educated at Leamington High School and the Ecole Normale, Orleans, she went on to London University, where she obtained her B.A. in Modern Languages, and Cambridge Training College for Teachers. Her first post was at Bradford Girls' Grammar School, and from 1907 to 1915 she was teaching at the North London Collegiate School where the pioneering Miss Buss had been Headmistress. Whilst there she took her M.A. in History by thesis at London University in her spare time. From 1915 to 1922 she was Headmistress of Twickenham County School. In January 1922 she was selected from forty-one candidates to become Headmistress of the King's High School for Girls, Warwick, taking up the post at the beginning of the summer term.

Miss Doorly was a most successful headmistress. The number of pupils rose from 361 to 523 within a few years. She was a tall commanding figure, with a faithful Alsatian dog named Vlah (Albanian for friendship), and is still remembered with affection by the older old girls. She was nicknamed 'Aunt Do' because she advised the girls to think of her as an aunt.

At the outset she introduced School and Form Councils and a Parent-Teacher Association, bodies accepted without question today but regarded as revolutionary at the time. By means of the School Council, composed of both staff and pupils, not only the prefects but representatives from each form could make their grievances known, and, although the Headmistress had the ultimate power of veto, at least the pupils felt they had some say in running the school.

She sought to train girls for university, although 'blue stockings' were

Eleanor Doorly in the ancient garden at the rear of Landor House, Warwick.

not encouraged. She was not only a brilliant linguist; she stimulated the girls' interest in art and music and current affairs. She seemed to know many important people and among those she persuaded to address the school were such as Gilbert Murray, John Galsworthy, Alfred Noyes, Laurence Housman, John Drinkwater and Ronald Ross. Recitals were given by prominent musicians such as the violinist Jelly d'Aranyi. Every Wednesday morning she arranged a lecture for the whole school. Sometimes it would be a visiting speaker, but as likely as not it was she herself who gave the talks on a variety of topics.

Eleanor Doorly retired to Dartmouth at Christmas 1944 at the age of 64 and died there on May 2nd 1950. An appreciation in the "Warwick Advertiser" at the time of her retirement commented: "It is almost impossible to begin to thank her for the beauty, the vitality, the breadth she has brought into the life of the school, for the courage needed to introduce so many of her reforms, for the help and advice she has given so generously to two decades of girls." Old Girls "will always remember her with admiration, gratitude and affection."

— 27 —

New Testament Scholar

C .H. (Charles Harold) Dodd, C.H., D.D., a man with recurring Ds and the same initials after his name as in front, was one of our foremost New Testament scholars. He was born in Wrexham in 1884, the son of a schoolmaster. He went up to University College, Oxford, where he gained a First Class Honours degree in Classics, and went on to train for the Congregational ministry at Mansfield College. Whilst at 'Univ.' he coxed the college boat which collided with the Pembroke boat in which the future 'Red Dean', Hewlett Johnson, was rowing, causing it to sink!

In his diary for January 21st 1912 Dodd recorded: "Preached at Brook Street Congregational Church, Warwick morning and evening. In the afternoon visited Sunday School and heard Countess of Warwick at Pleasant Sunday Afternoon." On February 6th he recorded: "Received call from Warwick." The call was accepted, lodgings were booked at No.23 West Street and in April he was ordained and welcomed to the pastorate of Brook Street.

Warwick proved to be an ideal setting for the young bachelor's only experience of an extended pastoral ministry. He quickly commended himself to the people of Warwick and gained warm attachments to many families in his Brook Street congregation. An inveterate walker he explored much of the countryside around Warwick. He stayed $3^1/2$ years until he returned to Mansfield to succeed Dr. James Moffatt as tutor in September 1915, but when the college was temporarily closed because of the War, he returned to Warwick from January 1918 until April 1919.

Dodd remained at Mansfield until 1930 when he succeeded another great Biblical scholar, A.S. Peake, as Rylands Professor of Biblical Criticism at the University of Manchester. In 1936 he began thirteen years as Norris-Hulme Professor of Divinity at the University of Cambridge, the first Free Churchman to hold an Oxbridge divinity chair. At various times he was also Sarum Lecturer at Oxford, Shaffer Lecturer at Yale, Ingersoll Lecturer at Harvard, Stone Lecturer at Princeton and Bampton Lecturer at Columbia. Besides which, he was a first-rate broadcaster, a strong advocate of the reunion of the Churches (he just lived to see the formation of the United Reformed Church in 1972) and the author of more than twenty books including "The Founder of Christianity" and "The Interpretation of the Fourth Gospel".

But his greatest work was accomplished between 1950 and 1970 as Director of that monumental work of scholarship, the New English Bible. He was made a Companion of Honour in 1963 after the publication of the New Testament, and the climax of his career came in March 1970 at the age of nearly 86 when he formally received copies of the N.E.B. from the publishers in Westminster Abbey, handed them to representatives of the sponsoring churches and societies, and gave a presentation copy to the Queen Mother.

C.H. Dodd died in September 1973 at the age of 89. He was honoured in the following January at a memorial service in the Abbey, an historic and unique event for a Free Church minister. The Dean summed up the feelings of a distinguished and representative congregation: "He belonged to all of us who bear the name of Christ. Every part of Christ's Church is a debtor to him." And he would, no doubt, be the first to acknowledge his debt to those early years in Warwick.

— 28 —

The Hobbit

J.R.R. (John Roland Reuel) Tolkien is well-known for his whimsical "Hobbit" and "The Lord of the Rings". What is not so well known is that his books were inspired by that part of the Warwickshire countryside which is now suburban Birmingham.

Tolkien was born in 1892 in Bloemfontein in the Orange Free State where his father was a bank manager. He was brought back to England – to Kings Heath – by his mother, the daughter of a Birmingham draper, in 1895. After his father's death in South Africa the following year he and his mother moved to No.5 Gracewell "in the hamlet of Sarehole", later No.264 Wake Green Road. Opposite was Sarehole Mill, its chimney-stack rising above the willow- and sedge-fringed pool. Coldbath Brook had turned the mill wheel here since mediaeval times, although the buildings as Tolkien knew them were rebuilt in 1773. The mill, since restored, now stands as a working museum.

Sarehole territory, already under threat of urbanisation by 1900, was the inspiration for Tolkien's rural 'Shire' being destroyed by barbarism. In 1900 they moved to a house in Moseley Road, and from it Tolkien could see the industry and housing of Small Heath and Sparkbrook, the 'Moloch' threatening his Shire. Another move followed to a house behind Kings Heath railway station, where he became fascinated with the Welsh place-names on passing coal-wagons – his earliest acquaintance with the philology which was to become his life's work.

Tolkien was educated at King Edward VI's School, Birmingham, and Exeter College, Oxford, where in 1915 he graduated with First Class Honours in English Language and Literature. He married Edith Bratt at Warwick the following year, and then as an officer of the Lancashire Fusiliers survived the horrors of the Somme. After the War (1920) he was appointed Reader in English Language at the University of Leeds. But most of his working life until his retirement in 1959 was spent at Oxford: in 1925 he was elected Rawlinson and Bosworth Professor of Anglo-Saxon and in 1945 Merton Professor of English Language and Literature. He also had a remarkable knowledge of Welsh, Finnish, Icelandic and Germanic languages.

However the major scholarly works which were expected of him failed to materialise. His energies were absorbed instead in the writing of fiction – recognised by a recent Waterstone's poll which heralds "The Lord of the Rings" as "The Book of the Century".

Tolkien died in 1973 at the age of 81.

— 29 —

Sugar Mummy

COUNTESS Markiewicz may have been the first woman elected to the House of Commons in 1918; Lady Astor the first to take her seat in 1919; and the Countess of Warwick the first to fight a Warwickshire constituency in 1923; but Mavis Tate in 1931 was probably the first woman M.P. with Warwickshire connections, albeit briefly, as mistress of Billesley Manor.

Billesley is a small parish on the north side of the Stratford-Alcester road. The village has long since disappeared. The early seventeenth century hall which has late eighteenth and twentieth century additions is still there as the four-star Billesley Manor Hotel, as is All Saints Church, still consecrated but in the care of the Redundant Churches Fund. But the process of depopulation probably began as long ago as the Black Death – the visitation of 1361 was particularly severe in this part of Warwickshire – and it was certainly hastened by the enclosures of the fifteenth century. About 1450 John Rous lamented the utter decay of the village, of which even then nothing was left but the manor house.

Successive halls, however, survived, and among the owners of the manor were Sir William Trussell who was involved in the death of Piers Gaveston in 1312, Sir Robert Lee who was Lord Mayor of London in 1602 - 03, and Dr. Thomas Sherlock who was Bishop of London from 1748 to 1761.

Shakespeare is said to have made use of its library and to have written "As You Like It" here. Certainly his grand-daughter Elizabeth Nash married her second husband in Billesley Church, and there are those who surmise that six coffins tantalisingly inaccessible in its hidden crypt may contain the mortal remains of the Bard and his relations.

Henry Burton ('Bertie') Tate, 'the Captain' to his tenantry, was owner of Billesley Manor from 1912 to 1927. He was the son of the founder of the Tate and Lyle sugar empire and donor of the Tate Gallery. He was to divorce his first wife Elizabeth who became Lady Lyttleton of Studley Manor, and to marry as his second wife Mavis Constance, the daughter of Guy Weir Hogg and former wife of Gerald Ewart Gott.

'The Captain' gave magnificent Christmas parties to his tenants in the Hall. At Christmas 1926 presents were given out to them all by Mavis as the new 'missus'. She is remembered as "a good looker, slender and tall, but

Billesley Manor.

somewhat severe and a bit abrupt. She had an air of mystery about her and when roused could use a lashing tongue." The following summer, presumably influenced by Mavis, the Captain decided to sell out and move to London, and they finally settled near Box in Wiltshire.

Mavis became a Justice of the Peace and was also very interested in politics. She contested Islington in the L.C.C. election in March 1931, and then became a Conservative M.P. for fourteen years. She entered Parliament as M.P. for West Willesden in 1931 when she had a majority of over 8,000, and transferred to the Frome division of Somerset in 1935 when she was one of only nine women returned. This time her majority was just under a thousand, and in Labour's landslide victory of 1945 she lost her Frome seat by five and a half thousand votes. She had a strong social conscience, and volunteered to be a member of the Parliamentary delegation which saw at first hand the horrors of Belsen concentration camp when it was liberated. Unfortunately, the enormity of what she had seen preyed on her mind, and as a result she committed suicide on June 5th 1947, a tragic end to the life of the Sugar Mummy of Billesley Manor.

— 30 —

Olympic Athlete

AT the Berlin Olympic Games of 1936 at which the coloured Jesse Owens so annoyed Hitler with his athletic prowess, a former Warwick School lad, Godfrey Brown, won the Silver Medal for Britain in the 400 metres and the Gold in the 1600 metres relay. He went on to win further Gold Medals in the 400 metres in the World Student Games in the following year and in the European Championships in 1938.

The story of how he came to Warwick, befriended by a complete stranger, is most interesting. His father, Rev. Arthur Brown, was a Methodist missionary who had stayed with Miss Emily Broadbent, a member of Northgate Methodist Church, when he came to Warwick to preach on Foreign Missions. When he was shortly due to return to Bengal, followed by his wife, he told Miss Broadbent that they were worried about what to do with the seven-year-old because he was too old to return to India with them but too young to go to boarding school. Miss Broadbent had recently been left alone by the death of her aunt, Maria Collins, and she amazed everyone by offering to 'adopt' the boy. Accordingly his mother left him at No.82 Emscote Road in October 1922 and he continued to live there during school terms until 1934, Miss Broadbent acting as a foster-mother for what Godfrey Brown has himself described as "twelve very happy and fulfilling years". She was, of course, no relation, but he called her 'aunt' for convenience – and in retrospect regarded her as a saint.

Godfrey Brown went on to Peterhouse College, Cambridge, and then served as an assistant master at Bedford School, King's School, Rochester, and Cheltenham College. He became Headmaster of the Royal Grammar School, Worcester from 1950 to 1978, and the small boy, who used to count the panes of glass in the windows of the Methodist church during boring sermons, was invited back to take the chair at a Rally at Northgate in 1951 to celebrate 150 years of Methodism in the town. Latterly he lived in retirement in Sussex and died in February 1995 just short of his 80th birthday.

— 31 —

Yorkshire Author

J.B.Priestley is regarded as the quintessential gruff Yorkshireman, and yet he spent all his adult life further south, including his last twenty-four years in Warwickshire.

Novelist, playwright, essayist, journalist, broadcaster and popular historian and sociologist, John Boynton Priestley was born in Bradford on September 13th 1894. His father was a schoolmaster and a Baptist. When he was only two years old his mother died and he was brought up by a loving stepmother. At sixteen he left the local grammar school and took a job as a clerk in a woollen firm. He volunteered when war broke out, served in Flanders, was wounded twice and finally commissioned. After the War he went up to Trinity Hall, Cambridge, to read English and History, and then became a free-lance writer and book reviewer. Novels followed – "Adam in Moonshine", "Benighted", "The Good Companions" (his most famous) and "Angel Pavement" (generally regarded as his finest). "The Good Companions", a warm-hearted tale of a travelling theatrical troupe, came out at the time of the Wall Street crash of 1929 and according to one witness "soared out of the gloom like a fairy tale to lift thousands of minds into a world of literary enchantment". It was to become one of the biggest best-sellers of the century.

Other novels followed over the years – "Daylight on Saturday", "Festival at Farbridge" and "Lost Empires" – and in all he was to write fifty books of various kinds, twenty-five plays and innumerable essays. He published his first play, "Dangerous Corner", in 1932. Others included "Time and the Conways", "When We Are Married", "An Inspector Calls" and "The Linden Tree", and it is a sign of his continuing popularity that his dramas are still performed from time to time.

Priestley was also a popular sociologist. His "English Journey", under-taken in the autumn of 1933, published the following year, and since reissued and televised, bears the sub-title "A Rambling but Truthful Account of What One Man Saw and Heard and Felt and Thought during a Journey through England", and it attempted to discover and describe how the economic crisis of the 1930s affected England. But it was the approach of war once more that completed the transformation of this bluff and cantankerous yet kindly pipe-smoking family man into the representative of the average Englishman.

On September 3rd 1939 he broadcast his first instalment of "Let the People Sing", and then in the dark days between June and October 1940 he delivered heartening patriotic "Postscripts" after the peak period of the nine o'clock news on a Sunday evening, "Postscripts" which were listened to by between 30 and 40 per cent of the adult population. He rivalled Churchill. (The "Guardian"'s tongue-in-cheek 'Pass Notes' recently said he "Won Battle of Britain with Wilfred Pickles"!) Indeed Priestley believed the broadcasts excited Churchill's jealousy, and when the B.B.C. in its mysterious way dropped him, he thought the Prime Minister was responsible, though it was more probably Conservative Central Office, suspicious of his left-wing views. Though he was never a party man – he stood (unsuccessfully) as an Independent candidate for Cambridge University in 1945 – he contributed regular essays to the magazines "John Bull" and "New Statesman"; he was credited along with the "Daily Mirror" and the Left Book Club for the size of the Labour Party's large majority in 1945; and he even made an official Labour election broadcast in 1950. And it was a Priestley article in the "New Statesman" in 1957 which led directly to the formation of the Campaign for Nuclear Disarmament.

Priestley's writings made him wealthy and he became a bon viveur. Modest homes in Oxfordshire and Highgate, North London (a house once lived in by Samuel Taylor Coleridge), were succeeded by an apartment in Central London and by more up-market residences in the Isle of Wight, the second of which was an estate with two dairy farms – before he finally moved to Kissing Tree House in the village of Alveston near Stratford-upon-Avon with his third wife Jacquetta Hawkes.

Priestley was very much a ladies' man. He and his first wife Pat had two daughters. He met his future second wife Jane (herself estranged from her first husband whom she subsequently divorced) and they had a daughter while Pat was dying of cancer. After marrying he and Jane had another daughter and a son. Their 27-year marriage was alternately affectionate and stormy, with periodic separations and unfaithfulness on his part – though the young Peggy Ashcroft resisted all his blandishments.

In his mid-fifties Priestley fell in love again with another man's wife. Literary co-operation with archaeologist Jacquetta Hawkes developed into much more. In the much publicised divorce case brought by Professor Hawkes in 1953, Priestley as co-respondent was lambasted by the judge. Yet, against all public expectations, his third marriage to Jacquetta Hawkes, lasting till his death 31 years later, proved to be very happy and faithful. And Jane's third marriage also lasted 25 happy years.

Kissing Tree House is a large white Regency mansion standing in its own grounds in beautiful countryside, and in its library Priestley received a constant stream of guests and interviewers. Ironically the house was later occupied by millionaire salesman John Fenton who actually ran Priestley Centenary Celebrations to raise funds for the Conservative Party!

Priestley's most significant writings appeared before he moved to Alveston in 1960, but his "Literature and Western Man" was published that year and his autobiography "Margin Released" two years later. He successfully adapted Iris Murdoch's novel "A Severed Head" as a play, and in 1969 - 72 he produced an historical trilogy dealing with the century from 1815 to 1919 - "The Prince of Pleasure", "Victoria's Heyday" and "The Edwardians". His last book, written at Kissing Tree House, was his autobiographical "Instead of the Trees", appearing in 1977.

At various times Priestley turned down political honours – a knighthood and two offers of a peerage – but he accepted appointment to the exclusive Order of Merit. He also accepted a clutch of honorary degrees – and in 1973 the Freedom of his native Bradford.

He died at Kissing Tree House on August 14th 1984, and a memorial service was held in Westminster Abbey for a great writer who had left the world a richer place than he found it.

— 32 —

The Man who Chopped India in Half

F EW people today remember Sir Cyril Radcliffe. Indeed few people at the time were aware of his existence. He was a civil servant, and civil servants for the most part go about their work quietly and anonymously, even when you chop a continent in half. For Sir Cyril was the man who mapped the boundary between India and Pakistan which resulted in the migration of fifteen million people and the deaths of perhaps a million.

Cyril Radcliffe was born in 1899 and educated at Haileybury and New College, Oxford, where he became a Fellow of All Souls. A brilliant career in the law resulted in him becoming a King's Counsel in 1935 at the early age of 36. Then during the War he was drafted into the Civil Service where he became the Director-General of the Ministry of Information from 1941 to 1945.

There followed his Indian episode, after which he was made a Life Peer on his appointment as a Law Lord in 1949, being advanced to Viscount in 1962. He was Reith Lecturer in 1951; he collected some seven honorary degrees from various universities; and before his death in 1977 he periodically hit the headlines as Chairman of a number of bodies – the Royal Commission on the Taxation of Profits and Income, the B.B.C. General Advisory Council, the Inquiry into Security Procedures and Practices, the Inquiry into the Vassall Case, the Inquiry into D Notices, the Committee on Memoirs of ex-Ministers, and, not least, the Board of Trustees of the British Museum.

But to quote the *Guardian* newspaper, "It was his fateful passage to India in July 1947, and his labours as the Raj's midnight gravedigger, that secured him a place in the history books."

Just before British rule in India was to end on August 15th 1947, Radcliffe was sent there as Chairman of the Bengal and Punjab Boundary Commissions, and his hasty amateur map-making was to result in the greatest movement of population in human history. To be fair to him, however, following the unprecedented demand for Indian independence during the War, both the British Government in London and Mountbatten as Viceroy on the spot wanted to be shot of the sub-continent as soon as possible.

Radcliffe had little inkling what he was letting himself in for, or what would be the baleful result of his work. He had no specialised knowledge of India: indeed, his lack of it was deemed an asset by those who appointed him, a guarantee of impartiality. He had assumed that he would merely have to adjudicate over disputes arising from the boundaries of Bengal and the Punjab. In fact it was a thankless task of far greater proportions – neither province with its mixture of Muslims, Hindus and Sikhs could be allocated as a whole to either India or Pakistan, nor were there any obvious lines of separation. Moreover, although he had been led to believe that he would have at least six months to complete the job, he was in fact given only 36 days to pore over a sheaf of maps and the volumes of the 1941 Census of India! But in the hot Indian summer he did his best – despite the fact that the reticent Radcliffe and the outgoing Mountbatten didn't get on together.

In the event the two new nations of India and Pakistan did not know where their boundaries were until Independence Day – and those boundaries have been disputed ever since.

In retrospect Radcliffe realised that he had been given an impossible task. He wrote, "No one in India will love me for the award about the

Hampton Lucy House.

Punjab and Bengal, and there will be roughly 80 million people with a grievance who will begin looking for me. I do not want them to find me." And some years after Partition he commented, "People sometimes ask me whether I would like to go back and see India as it really is. God forbid. Not even if they asked me. I suspect they'd shoot me out of hand – both sides."

And the local connection? Radcliffe lived at Hampton Lucy House, a Queen Anne mansion with six main bedrooms and five attics. Francis Smith ("Smith of Warwick") and his brother had built the house as a rectory. It had been commissioned by Dr. William Lucy who took over the living on inheriting Charlecote. He had the family mansion to live in and built the rectory as a house for his impecunious nephew who was to be his curate.

Warwickshire honoured Lord Radcliffe. He was a Trustee of the Shakespeare Birthplace Trust and Chancellor of the University of Warwick who awarded him one of his honorary degrees of Doctor of Literature.

— 33 —

The Leamington Licker

ON July 10th 1951 Randolph Turpin of Leamington astonished the boxing world by beating the great Sugar Ray Robinson to bring the middle-weight championship of the world to Britain for the first time in the twentieth century. His was a rags to riches story – and then back to rags again. Only fifteen years later he was apparently to commit suicide.

Randy was the youngest of the three boxing sons (the others were Dick and Jackie) of Lionel Turpin who came from what was then British Guiana, settled here after serving in France in the First World War and married a local girl whose father had been a bare-knuckle fighter. Of the elder brothers, Dick became British and Empire middle-weight champion, and died in 1990 at the age of 69.

Randolph Turpin was born on June 7th 1928. His first home was a damp shoddy basement in Willes Road, Leamington. Before he was a year old his father died and his mother moved to Warwick where the family finally went to live in Wathen Road when his mother remarried. He attended Westgate School in the town. Always in scrapes as a youngster, he learnt to box at Leamington Boys' Club and won a number of schoolboy boxing championships. After leaving school he worked for Alderman Bill Tarver, a local builder – work that involved swinging a pick which helped to develop that knock-out hook that flattened some of the best boxers in the ring. He won five titles as an amateur and then turned professional while doing his National Service in the Navy.

After training in the Nelson gymnasium above the gelatine factory in Warwick, Turpin gained his first professional title in October 1950 when he knocked out Albert Finch in the fifth round to gain the British middle-weight title which his brother Dick had lost to the same Albert Finch the year before. The following February the European middle-weight title was his as a result of a 48 seconds knock out of Lucien Van Dam of Holland. Then in July – as already mentioned – he surprised everyone by outpointing the title-holder Sugar Ray Robinson at Earl's Court, winning twelve of the fifteen rounds, to take the World middle-weight title. The "Leamington Licker" was to win other titles later on, but this was the peak of his career: he was never to be so convincing afterwards.

On that occasion he returned to his native town to a hero's welcome: he rode in a limousine between the Mayors of Leamington and Warwick (the latter was the Earl of Warwick) to a civic reception at Leamington Town

Hall. Thousands of people waited to cheer him as he appeared on the Town Hall balcony and that same evening a private dinner was given in his honour by the two mayors at the Manor House Hotel.

Yet only two months later he was to lose the title in a return fight with Sugar Ray in New York when the referee stopped the fight in the tenth round to save him from serious injury. However he was still British and European middle-weight champion, and in June 1952 he added the British and Empire light-heavy weight titles as well by beating the holder Don Cockell in the eleventh round when the fight was stopped with Cockell helpless on the ropes. And before the end of 1952 a fifth title, the Empire middle-weight, had come his way when he beat George Angelo on points.

Alas, from now onwards Turpin's career was to be less impressive. His

Randolph Turpin

next few years were full of 'downs' as well as 'ups'. These were doubtless influenced by a number of contributory factors: his cavalier attitude towards training; the break-up of his first marriage; a court case brought against him by an American woman alleging common assault; and a failed business venture as the joint owner of the Great Orme Hotel at Llandudno.

1953 was a turning point. At the end of 1952 the World middle-weight title was declared vacant because Robinson had not complied with the rule that a champion must defend his title every six months. To clear the way for a tilt at this title Randy gave up his two light-heavy weight titles and then defeated Charles Humez of France at the White City in an admittedly unimpressive points win in a European elimination bout. But when he met the United States champion Carl 'Bobo' Olsen at Madison Square Gardens in New York in October 1953 for the vacant world title, he disappointed his supporters by losing on points: he looked tired and weary and battered, "a strange Turpin," said one writer, "one who flattered to deceive." He had, it appeared, turned very temperamental in training, and this obviously had not helped.

Thereafter it was a case of swings and roundabouts. In May 1954 Turpin lost his European middle-weight title to Tiberio Mitri in Rome: the referee intervened in the very first round because Turpin had been knocked down and dazed and was not fit to continue. In April 1955 he regained the British and Empire light-heavy weight titles with a second round knock-out of Alex Buxton – only to be promptly knocked out himself the following October by outsider George Wallace in the fourth round. Yet in 1956 he came back to beat Buxton again to win back the British light-heavy weight title which he had twice before relinquished. He managed to survive several more fights until he finally retired after being knocked out in the second round by Yolande Pompey in Birmingham in September 1958.

Latterly Randolph Turpin had lived in St. Mary's Road, Leamington with his second wife Gwen and their family, and then in Russell Street where his wife ran a transport café and he cooked for the lorry drivers who ate there. Most of the considerable £300,000 fortune he had grossed during his career had gone: he had no sense of the value of money (for example, he bought five houses and several cars); he would not take financial advice; and he was too generous to sponging 'friends' who proceeded to desert him when he was down on his luck. He earned a little as a professional wrestler, but in 1962 the Inland Revenue filed a bankruptcy petition against him for £17,000 unpaid tax, and in June 1964 Leamington Corporation made a compulsory purchase order for the café because the site was needed for a car park. On May 17th 1966, three days after receiving another income tax demand, he was found shot in an upstairs room. The inquest jury returned a verdict of suicide, though doubts have since been raised. A promising life had ended tragically. Few personalities from the world of boxing attended the funeral. As the vicar said, "When his fame and fortune were gone, he was deserted."

— 34 —

Talented Actress

D O you remember the B.B.C.'s splendid black and white television production of Galsworthy's "Forsyte Saga" back in 1967, with Eric Porter as Soames, the Man of Property? Do you recall the Forsyte aunts, in particular Aunt Juley, the little tactless one who rescued a dog in the park and brought it back home to the consternation of the rest of the family? That cameo part was played by Nora Nicholson who was born in Leamington.

Her father was Irish and her mother from the Westcountry. They lived at Svea Lodge, No.42 Binswood Avenue. Father was the incumbent of St. Alban the Martyr in Warwick Street, a privately owned church with a copper spire situated at the junction with Portland Street where an office block now stands. It was ritualistic High Church, and significantly Nora became a Roman Catholic in later life.

Initially she was educated at home by her father; then she went for a year or two to Leamington High School; and finally she was sent to a boarding school in Bournemouth. She had always wanted to act. At her first audition at the Shakespeare Memorial Theatre Frank Benson grudgingly said, "It might be worth your while." However she was not daunted. She entered the Benson School and began auspiciously in his touring company as Puck, as one of the Princes in the Tower in "Richard III", a glorious one night stand as Juliet, and as Dolly in Bernard Shaw's "You Never Can Tell". This thorough grounding took her to the Old Vic and to an association with many of the most distinguished actors and playwrights of the day – Sybil Thorndike, Lewis Casson and John Gielgud, T.S. Eliot, Christopher Fry and Noel Coward. She sang for concert parties and stooged for comedians, and her versatility (hence the title of her autobiography "Chameleon's Dish") led her to play such Shakespearean parts as Ariel and Titania, Jessica and Desdemona, and one of the witches in "Macbeth", and to act in a wide variety of other plays – "The Cherry Orchard", "Trelawny of the Wells", "The Corn is Green", "The School for Scandal", "The Lady's not for Burning" and "The Family Reunion". Besides acting in the West End and in the provinces, she toured the United States, Canada and elsewhere. She appeared in films such as "The Blue Lagoon", "A Town like Alice" and "Fools Rush In". She appeared in radio programmes – and on television as early as February 1937 at the 'Ally Pally' in Noel Coward's "Hands across the Sea". She considered her favourite part of all time was Juno in Sean O'Casey's "Juno and the Paycock", but she really won her way into people's hearts with her portrayal of eccentric old ladies. There was old nanny, Nursie, in Alan Bennett's boy's school play "Forty Years On", and she confessed that one of the happiest engagements of her career was acting in Coward's "Waiting in the Wings", a story of a group of elderly actresses living in retirement. But it is as the Forsyte's Aunt Juley that most of us will remember the little old lady from Leamington.

— 35 —

Oxford Biochemist

SOME sixty years ago a young research student published her first paper. She went on to become one of the greatest scientists of the twentieth century, a leading peace campaigner and a successful wife and mother! Her name: Professor Dorothy Hodgkin. Her achievements: solving the structures of cholesterol, penicillin, vitamin B12 and insulin.

With a Quaker background Dorothy Mary Crowfoot was born on May 12th 1910 in Cairo where her father was in the Egyptian Ministry of Education. During the First World War the family returned to England and Dorothy was educated at Beccles in Suffolk (she was later to be honoured as the first Freeman of that town) and she was top of her year in the whole country in the School Certificate examination. She went up to Somerville College, Oxford, to study Chemistry and graduated with First Class Honours. Afterwards she went to Cambridge to get her Ph.D. and then returned to Oxford as Tutor in Chemistry at Somerville, specialising in crystallography. In the 1930s the University still restricted the proportion of women students to one in five of the numbers of men, yet Dorothy Crowfoot was able to set up her own X-ray crystallography laboratory, and within a year or two was supervising two male research students. She became a Fellow of Somerville in 1936 and remained as such until her retirement in 1977, then continuing as an Honorary Fellow. She became a Fellow of the Royal Society in 1947 at the early age of 37; she was the Royal Society's first Wolfson Research Professor from 1960 to 1977; she was awarded their Royal and Copley medals and was a member of many international learned societies.

In 1937 Dorothy Crowfoot married Thomas Hodgkin and they had two sons and a daughter. Her husband became Director of Extra-Mural Studies at Oxford, and later held a post at the University of Accra in Ghana where she visited him one term in three.

During the Second World War Dorothy worked on the structure of penicillin, making the first use of a computer in tackling a biochemical problem. In 1956 she discovered the molecular structure of vitamin B12, the factor used in the treatment of pernicious anaemia, and in 1969 she finally cracked insulin which she had first photographed more than thirty years before. How did she do it all?

Well, to quote Georgina Ferry,

"She has reserves of intelligence, practical competence, determination, cheerfulness, compassion, modesty, and most other desirable personal attributes that few people of either sex could hope to match in several lifetimes. To say that her career proves that women don't have problems getting on in science is like saying that the example of her student Margaret Roberts proves that women don't have problems getting on in politics.

That comparison raises further questions. Margaret Thatcher's strategy for success involved adopting essentially male characteristics – not for nothing was she portrayed by the satirical puppet show 'Spitting Image' in a man's pinstripe suit. In contrast, most of the many affectionate tributes to Professor Hodgkin that have been published refer to her essentially feminine qualities. Her example is a lesson that should be taken to heart by all budding scientists, male or female – and, more importantly, by those who fund research. Science doesn't have to be competitive, and scientists don't have to be ruthlessly singleminded to succeed."

Dorothy Hodgkin adopted an egalitarian approach to her work, insisting on first names and believing in collaboration rather than dictation. One result is the number of women in crystallography today, many of them her former students or junior staff. She used to hum for encouragement when the work was frustrating, and one of her former students commented, "The nicest time I remember her humming was when I suddenly realised that what was being hummed was 'Through the night of doubt and sorrow' – that was actually quite supportive!"

The Dorothy Hodgkin stamp.

Although she officially retired in 1977, Professor Hodgkin continued for many years to produce papers in collaboration with colleagues at Oxford and elsewhere, and she was regarded with enormous affection, particularly in the Third World, whose scientists she greatly encouraged. By this time she had long been a leading figure in the peace movement: along with Einstein and Bertrand Russell she was one of the founders of Pugwash in 1957, the group of scientists from East and West opposed to nuclear weapons who had originally met at the village of that name in Nova Scotia. She was awarded the Lenin Peace Prize in 1987.

She had many other honours showered upon her. Besides Somerville she had been a Fellow of Wolfson College, Oxford, and she became an Honorary Fellow of Linacre, Oxford, and of Girton and Newnham, Cambridge. From 1970 to 1988 she was Chancellor of Bristol University, and she was awarded honorary degrees by the Universities of Oxford, Cambridge, Bristol, Leeds, Manchester, York, Dalhousie, Modena and Zagreb. But perhaps the greatest honours that came to her were the Nobel Prize and the Order of Merit. She became only the third woman to win the Nobel Prize for Chemistry in 1964, following in the footsteps of Marie Curie and Irene Joliot-Curie – and, indeed, she is the *only* British woman ever to have won a Nobel prize for science. Characteristically, she decided to use the prize money for a scholarship and for the cause of peace and the relief of famine. The following year, 1965, she became only the second woman (after Florence Nightingale) to be appointed to the prestigious Order of Merit. In 1996 the Post Office chose her as the scientist in a "Famous Women" series: her portrait appeared on the 20p. stamp alongside a molecular model.

And the local connection? Professor Dorothy Hodgkin chose to spend the many years of her retirement — if you can call them that – at Crab Mill in the south Warwickshire village of Ilmington. Her husband died in 1982 and her long and useful life ended on July 29th 1994.

— 36 —

From Labourer's Son to Cabinet Minister

FREDERICK William Mulley rose from humble beginnings to become a Cabinet Minister. A labourer's son, he was born in Clemens Street, Leamington, on July 3rd 1918 and attended Bath Place Church of England School before winning a scholarship to Warwick School. His first job was as an insurance clerk in Waterloo Place for the local health insurance committee, and it was to be as a representative of these clerical workers that he owed his standing in the Labour Party. When war broke out he joined the Worcestershire Regiment and became a Lance-Sergeant before being captured at Dunkirk in 1940. He was a prisoner-of-war in Germany and Poland for the duration, but he put those five years to good use with studies which gained him a B.Sc. in Economics and recognition as a Chartered Secretary.

On repatriation Mulley won an adult scholarship to Christ Church, Oxford, where he obtained a First Class Honours degree in Philosophy, Politics and Economics in 1947. There followed a Research Studentship at Nuffield College, and then from 1948 to 1950 he was a Research Fellow in Economics at St. Catherine's College, Cambridge, where he also studied Law. Consequently he was an M.A. of both universities and was called to the Bar in 1954.

In 1945 Mulley had contested the safe Conservative seat of Sutton Coldfield, but he was elected as Labour member for the Park division of Sheffield in 1950, a constituency he held continuously until 1983 when he was unfortunately deselected. He stepped on the bottom rung of the ladder of political promotion almost immediately, being appointed Parliamentary Private Secretary to the Minister of Works in the dying months of the Attlee administration.

He was to be high in the counsels of the Labour Party. He was a member of its National Executive Committee continuously, apart from two short breaks, from 1957 to 1980, and as Chairman of the Labour Party from 1974 to 1975 he strenuously tried to maintain party unity at a time when it was divided over Britain's membership of the E.E.C.. Reliable, if a trifle pedestrian, he was the grey, bespectacled epitome of the party in the 1960s and 1970s, and a member of the 1964-70 and 1974-79 Governments throughout.

A politician of considerable personal modesty who has been rather overlooked by historians – his more flamboyant contemporaries such as Barbara Castle and Richard Crossman are better remembered – he held a succession of important public offices: Minister for the Army, 1964-65; Minister of Aviation, 1965-67, when he defended the Concorde project; Minister of State at the Foreign Office, 1967-69; and Minister of Transport, 1969-70, and again when Labour regained power, 1974-75. He then became a Cabinet Minster as Secretary of State for Education, 1975-76, when he was involved in the comprehensive versus grammar school dispute, and Secretary of State for Defence, 1976-79. It was in this latter capacity that in August 1977, after an exhausting night at the House of Commons, he momentarily nodded off whilst watching a Silver Jubilee R.A.F. fly-past sitting next to the Queen – an event unmercifully caught by press photographers! Subsequently, the expression "I am off to take a short Mulley" was said to have gained currency in officers' messes!

Both Harold Wilson and James Callaghan found Mulley unswervingly loyal. A right-wing pro-Marketeer, he played his part in the early days of both the Council of Europe and the Western European Union, being President of the latter from 1980 to 1983.

Our Leamington lad was created a life peer in 1984 and died on March 15th 1995. At his request he was buried beside his parents in the churchyard at Whitnash, just south of Leamington.

— 37 —

Racehorse Trainer

MERCY Cockburn was born in June 1919 and baptised in Northgate Methodist Church, Warwick. She was the daughter of Samuel Crosby Cockburn and his wife Elsie Simkin who lived at Budbrooke Lodge just outside the town and farmed some five hundred acres by the side of the Racecourse.

The little girl grew up with ponies and horses. She used to gallop through the streets of Warwick and would spend hours in the blacksmith's forge at the back of the Castle wall. On one occasion, going round a hairpin bend in Castle Lane, she fell off her pony and badly grazed herself but kept quiet about it because she was not supposed to gallop flat out on a hard surface. In any case she was meant to be in school! She got on well with her father but was in awe of a very strict mother. In fact Mrs. Cockburn 'used' her daughter. Mercy rode show ponies winning numerous championships, but her mother then sold them for substantial profits. Unlike other horsey children who grow up with their ponies, loving them for years even when they have outgrown them, Mercy's ponies were turned over double quick, sometimes even being sold on the showground. She had no sooner grown fond of a pony than it was whipped away from her. The one bonus for Mercy was that she got used to riding all sorts of horses.

At the age of 17 she was married in St. Mary's Collegiate Church, Warwick, to Fred Rimell who was to become four times National Hunt champion jockey between the 1938 – 39 and 1945 – 46 seasons. He broke his neck twice, and after the second occasion in 1947 he retired as a jockey to become a trainer at Kinnersley in Worcestershire. He worked for such owners as Sir George Dowty, Sir Edward Hanmer, Charles Hambro of Hambro's Bank and Paul ('Teazy-Weazy') Raymond. But if he trained the horses, Mercy did all the paper work, studied the form and decided in which races to enter the horses – steeds such as Comedy, Woodland Venture and Gaye Brief. The Rimell Stable won two Cheltenham Gold Cups, three Champion Hurdles and almost every other major race in the steeplechasing calendar. Most notably they won four Grand Nationals, more than anyone else at Aintree – with E.S.B. in 1956, Nicolaus Silver in 1961, Gay Trip in 1970 and Paul Raymond's Rag Trade in 1976.

On Fred's death in 1981, Mercy carried on as a trainer herself until she retired in 1989, having 232 winners in eight years.

And so the little girl once dominated by her mother had made it to the top of her profession.

— 38 —

The Hermit of Hull

NICKNAMED the "Hermit of Hull" because of his shyness and inaccessibility, the poet Philip Arthur Larkin was born on August 9th 1922 at No.2 Poultney Road in the Coventry suburb of Radford to Sydney and Eva Emily Larkin, an autocratic father and a submissive mother. Christened in the old Coventry Cathedral the lad came to be in awe of his father who became City Treasurer and an admirer of Hitler. When Philip was five years old the family moved to No. 1 Manor Road, near the city centre, an area demolished in the 1960s to make way for the inner ring road. For a shy boy in a dream world of his own, his childhood and adolescence were not particularly happy. He was educated at the King Henry VIII School in the city and then proceeded to St. John's College, Oxford. He did not apply himself wholeheartedly to his English studies, but affected to be unconventional and rebellious, drinking heavily, uttering obscenities in both speech and writing, and generally mocking authority. However, having been rejected for the army because of his poor eyesight, he was able to complete a wartime university course. By dint of a surge of last minute study he managed to get a First!

After the bombing of Coventry Philip's parents moved to Warwick in June 1941 – to No.73 Coten End, an early Victorian house which became his home in the vacations and where he had two attic rooms to himself. The Crown Hotel along the road became his watering hole, and it is ironic to think that only four years previously the house in which our bawdy and bibulous poet lived had been the Methodist manse!

The Larkins continued to live in Warwick until Mr. Larkin's death in 1948 and Mrs. Larkin moved to Leicester. Philip had been away from home since December 1943 when, having been rejected for the Civil Service, he became Librarian of a small public library in Wellington, Shropshire. Subsequently he became Sub-Librarian of University College, Leicester (1946 – 50), Sub-Librarian of Queen's University, Belfast (1950 – 55), and then for the last thirty years of his life (1955 – 85) the University Librarian of what came to be named the Brynmor Jones Library of the University of Hull.

Despite his natural indolence he threw himself into the work at Hull. During the first half of his time there he was responsible both for the

Philip Larkin

general conception and the detailed planning of a fine new extensive
library building, and throughout the tenure of his office he was a
successful library administrator at a time when both university and library
were undergoing colossal expansion: bookstock rose from 124,000 to half
a million, staff from a dozen to nearly a hundred, and students from 700
to 5,000. And it pained him when, in his last few years, he had to fight
against the cuts which came with the worsening economic situation. He
was also Secretary to the Hull University Press – he steered over a hundred
books, lectures and articles through to publication – and he was involved
in the life of the University in many other ways.

However, his great love was writing. Some of it was never published and
much of it was rather worthless, but it was all extremely personal. Much of
his poetry refers, obliquely perhaps, to actual incidents in his life,
describes his feelings for other people, especially his women friends, and
reflects his periods of both elation and depression:

"What, still alive at twenty-two,
  A fine upstanding lad like you?"

He was a complex character. There seemed to be two people in him – one
formal and reserved, the other spontaneous. Sedate on duty, he unwound

in private. For most of the 1970s an electric fuse-box high on the wall in one of the library's lavatories bore the legend "Knock three times and ask for Philip Larkin"! But the shy man who found it difficult to make friends was also the defiant writer who was not afraid to make enemies. All this is reflected in his writings. His published works included two novels, "Jill" (1946) and "A Girl in Winter" (1947), and two volumes of essays, "All What Jazz" (1970) and "Required Writing" (1983) which won the W.H.Smith Literary Award. Then there were his volumes of poetry, "The North Ship" (1945), "XX Poems" (1951), "The Less Deceived" (1955), his most famous volume "The Whitsun Weddings" (1964) and "High Windows" (1974). His biographer comments, ""The Less Deceived" made his name; "The Whitsun Weddings" made him famous; "High Windows" turned him into a national monument." He also completed the editing of "The Oxford Book of Twentieth Century English Verse" in 1973. His poems have appeared in various anthologies and his posthumous "Collected Poems" which appeared in 1988 contained hitherto unpublished material.

Larkin never married. He was essentially selfish – many artists are – and he thought that marriage and children would tie the hands of the writer within him, and that his opinion of the boring and pedestrian marriage of his parents was no recommendation for that institution.

> "They f— you up, your mum and dad.
> They may not mean to, but they do.
> They fill you with the faults they had
> And add some extra, just for you.
>
> Man hands on misery to man.
> It deepens like a coastal shelf.
> Get out as early as you can,
> And don't have any kids yourself."   ("This be the Verse")

And yet he could also write:

> "The trees are coming into leaf...
> In full grown thickness every May.
> Last year is dead, they seem to say,
> Begin afresh, afresh, afresh."   ("The Trees")

His aversion to marriage did not prevent Larkin having sexual relations, but such relations, if not disastrous, were at least difficult and at times turbulent. Shamefully, he got engaged to his first love, Ruth Bowman, who shared his love of literature, without seriously intending to marry her. Monica Jones, whom he met at Leicester, was to be his companion for over thirty-five years, though they kept their independent existences and she only moved in with him after a serious illness less then three years before his death. For many years he was two-timing with Maeve Brennan, a member of his staff, and lying to cover his tracks. Indeed for a short while he was three-timing with his secretary, Betty Mackereth – after he had already been with her every working day for seventeen years!

As the years went by, Larkin's heart gradually went out of his work. He drank even more heavily and he withdrew from many of his university commitments. In the last few years of his life he produced little poetry. Early in life he had become obsessed with death, and as time went on, without the consolation of religion, he presented a more pathetic figure. "What an absurd, empty life! And the grave yawns," he wrote in January 1975. One of his few offerings at this time concerns his accidental killing of a hedgehog while mowing the lawn:

> "The mower stalled, twice; kneeling, I found
> A hedgehog jammed up against the blades,
> Killed. It had been in the long grass.
>
> I had seen it before, and even fed it, once.
> Now I had mauled its unobtrusive world
> Unmendably. Burial was no help:
>
> Next morning I got up and it did not.
> The first day after a death, the new absence
> Is always the same; we should be careful
>
> Of each other, we should be kind
> While there is still time."   ("The Mower")

Honours were showered upon Larkin. He received honorary Doctorates of Literature from the Universities of Belfast, Leicester, Oxford, St. Andrews, Sussex, Warwick and the New University of Ulster. He won the Queen's Gold Medal for Poetry in 1965 and was made a C.B.E. in 1975. On Betjeman's death in December 1984 he was offered, but declined, the office of Poet Laureate (Ted Hughes was appointed instead). He declined partly out of shyness and partly because of his conviction that the muse of poetry had deserted him: he knew he could come up with lines to order, but he believed the Laureate should produce more than merely required writing for special occasions. A few months before his death he was made a Companion of Honour, but "spiralling down towards extinction" as he put it, he was unable to attend the investiture, and he died of cancer on December 2nd 1985, saying faintly, "I am going to the inevitable". A sad end for the Warwickshire man who has left his mark upon English literature.

— 39 —

Historian of the
Working Class

A S we have seen, G.M. Trevelyan was the greatest historian of the first half of the twentieth century, but who in retrospect will be seen as the most significant historian of the second half of this century? There is a formidable list of candidates. What about Hugh Trevor-Roper who as a young intelligence officer produced that masterpiece not of detective fiction but of detective fact, "The Last Days of Hitler"? Or Christopher Hill, Marxist Master of Balliol and doyen of seventeenth century scholars? Or A.L. Rowse, Fellow of All Souls and specialist in Tudor and Cornish history? And we must not forget A.J.P. Taylor whose extempore stand-up talks on television so helped to popularise history. Well, all of these have massive claims, but may I offer E.P. Thompson, historian of the working class and Reader in the Centre for the Study of Social History at the University of Warwick from 1965 to 1971?

"The Guardian" obituarist in August 1993 rightly regarded him as "part of a radical line running from John Bunyan to William Morris", who was in fact the subject of his first major work. Edward Palmer Thompson's life of dissent began on February 3rd 1924. He was the son of a former Methodist minister, Edward John Thompson and his wife Theodosia Jessup. Both his parents had been missionaries in India, but shortly before Edward was born his father left the ministry for a fellowship at Oriel College, Oxford, and a university lectureship in Bengali. Mahatma Gandhi and Pandit Nehru were among the steady flow of Indian visitors to their Oxford home – it is said that Nehru taught Edward how to hold a cricket bat properly. After the Dragon School in Oxford, he went to his father's old school, Kingswood School, Bath. But he was to reject the Christian faith and become a very concerned Communist.

Study at Corpus Christi, Cambridge, was divided by service as a tank commander in North Africa and Italy, and then from 1948 to 1965 Thompson was tutor in history and literature in the Extra-Mural Department of the University of Leeds. It was in 1963 whilst he was there that he produced the seminal work, "The Making of the English Working

Class". This demonstrates supremely the first of the two elements in E.P. Thompson's contribution to the history of the second half of the twentieth century – his turning upside down the writing of history. Essentially it is an approach to history from the bottom upwards instead of from the top down. It had not been altogether the fault of the older historians that their writing had adopted a 'kings and queens' approach: after all, nobles' castles had survived but villeins' hovels hadn't, and until the working class was literate there could be no working class sources. But to quote some oft-quoted words from Thompson's preface to the book: "I am seeking to rescue the poor stockinger, the Luddite cropper, the 'obsolete' hand-loom weaver, the 'utopian' artisan........from the enormous condescension of posterity." In the process his writing treats people, not as items in a statistical table, but as human beings, while the concurrent flowering of local history studies covering the lives of ordinary people complements his approach.

After Leeds, E.P.T. had those six years at Warwick University but resigned in 1971 after writing a stinging Penguin Special about the ethos and administrative arrangements of this new "business university" conveniently sited "in the mid-Atlantic of the motor industry". He then started a career as an independent writer and scholar.

Fifteen years previously he had left the Communist Party at the time of the Hungarian uprising of 1956 and become a dissident of the New Left opposed to both Stalin's heirs and the N.A.T.O. alliance. He felt that both sides were using the cold war to erode democratic freedoms and to transgress human rights. If the contribution of the disarmament movement to the end of the cold war has been ignored, so has Thompson's part in it as a founder of European Nuclear Disarmament and the writer of such polemical pieces as "Writing by Candlelight" and "Protest and Survive", the counterblast to the official "Protect and Survive". This was the other element in his contribution to contemporary history – his intervention in the politics of the cold war and his exposure of the policies of the nuclear deterrent – in a 1980s world which seemed to him to be more dangerous than it had been for several decades. As W.L. Webb wrote in "The Guardian", "It was an intervention which will one day be seen to be as much part of the moral history of his country as his historian's mission to rescue the lives and endeavours of the poor from the dark abyss of time in which the indifference or antagonism of establishment historians had been largely content to leave them." In other words, he helped to make history as well as write it.

The secular dissenter whose actions sprang from his upbringing in religious nonconformity died at his home near Worcester on August 28th 1993.

— 40 —

International Show-Jumper

THE secluded east Warwickshire village of Priors Marston has its own interesting local history. This village of 500 souls once had as many as four places of worship – Wesleyan and Primitive Methodist chapels as well as the parish church and a continuing Moravian chapel. Because of its proximity to Edgehill anecdotes about the Civil War abound. And who can forget the story of the time when the publican was also the bus driver and his dog did its courting in a neighbouring village regularly once a week because it knew it could get a lift back from its master on that particular day? But Priors Marston only really hit the headlines when it became the home of Caroline Bradley, perhaps the most complete horsewoman Britain has ever produced and, in the opinion of many, the finest lady showjumper in the world.

Caroline had a passion for ponies and horses from her earliest days: she could ride before she could walk, and as a schoolgirl she entered local Gymkhana, Pony Club, and hunter trials and events. Because she was technically classed as a professional she was never able to compete in the Olympics, but she represented her country on many occasions, and her fans will mention her in the same breath as Pat Smythe, Harvey Smith and David Broome. She made her international debut at Dublin in 1966 at the age of 20. She was Puissance Champion at the Horse of the Year Show at Wembley in 1974 and Leading Showjumper at the Horse of the Year Show in 1977 on Marius. The following year she won the Queen Elizabeth II Cup at the Royal International Horse Show, again on Marius, and two years later won it once more, this time on her favourite horse Tigre. In 1978 she took part in the World Championships at Aachen, helping the British team win a gold medal – and the World Championships, not the Olympics, are regarded as the ultimate test by most horsemen and women. No wonder she was Daily Express Sportswoman of the Year in 1979.

Besides taking a keen interest in Riding for the Disabled, Caroline continued to take part in all grades of shows. By this time she regularly took nine horses to a show and rode every one of them. On one occasion she rode fourteen in a day! Indeed she literally worked herself to death at the early age of 37. For besides all her showjumping and the myriad practices and preparations that entailed, she kept stables for up to thirty horses at Priors Marston, training and looking after other people's horses as well as her own. Her minimum working day was from six in the morning to nine at night, and, although she had a full complement of stable-girls, she insisted on doing much of the 'mucking-out' and other routine work herself. She also did her own paperwork and drove her own horse-box both in this country and abroad. Numerous falls brought her severe arthritis. In June 1983 she had just ridden into second place in the first round of the main jumping competition at the Suffolk Show. Dismounting in the collecting ring she complained of feeling unwell and crumpled to the ground. St. John Ambulance men were on hand to apply first aid, but Caroline died on the way to Ipswich Hospital.

Priors Marston remembers her with a simple tombstone in the churchyard.

Caroline Bradley's grave in Priors Marston Churchyard.

— 41 —

Phil Archer

WHO has a personal entry in the "Guinness Book of Records" for playing the most durable character in the world's longest-running daily radio serial? Norman Painting as Phil Archer. He has been with the Archers ever since their inception in 1951 and has written at least 1200 of the scripts himself, including No. 10,000 in 1989.

Norman George Painting was born on April 23rd 1924, the son of Harry George and Maud Painting, of No.28 Grove Street, Leamington. He was baptised in one Methodist church there (Trinity) and attended the Sunday School of another (Dale Street). He was educated at Leamington College for Boys, King Edward VI School, Nuneaton, and Birmingham University, where he obtained a First Class Honours degree. Apart from some time at Oxford as a tutor in Anglo-Saxon Language and Literature and ten years spent in London, Norman Painting has lived all his life in Warwickshire – in Leamington for his first fourteen years, in Wormleighton, in Rugby, and since 1967 in Warmington, where he lives in the old rectory, eighteenth century Warmington Grange, where, incidentally, you can find an old door salvaged from the former All Saints' Church at Emscote.

Awarded the O.B.E. in 1976, Norman Painting is very versatile. Besides radio scripts, he has written a best-selling "Forever Ambridge" (1975), has presented television films such as "One Man's Warwickshire", and has written poetry, serials and stage plays in his own name and as 'Philip Bentinck' and 'Bruno Milna'. He is a patron of many good causes and is associated with many local bodies. He is a Vice-President of St. Mary's Church, Warwick, a Vice-President of the Royal Pump Room Association, Leamington, and a Trustee and former Chairman of the Warwickshire and Coventry Historic Churches Trust. The Royal Agricultural Society of England has made him an Honorary Life Governor for his services to agriculture. He plays the organ at his local parish church, but his great love is a love of gardens. He has written numerous television documentaries on gardening subjects. As Patron of the Tree Council he was instrumental in setting up, in collaboration with the Shakespeare Birthplace Trust, the Shakespeare Tree Garden in Stratford, whose first tree was planted by the Queen Mother. And he takes great delight in his own extensive garden at Warmington Grange which he opens to the public under the National Gardens Scheme.

Bibliography

ALLEN, Joan – Heardred's Hill: a History of Hartshill and Oldbury (Bethany Enterprises, Nuneaton, 1982)

BENET, William Rose – The Reader's Encyclopaedia (Black, 2nd ed., 1965)

The Birmingham Evening Mail

The Birmingham Post

The Birmingham Post and Mail Year Book and Who's Who

BIRTLEY, Jack – The Tragedy of Randolph Turpin (New English Library, 1975)

BRIGDEN, Thomas E. – Notes on Some Warwick Worthies (Henry T. Cooke & Son, Warwick, 1895)

BROME, Vincent – J.B. Priestley (Hamish Hamilton, 1988)

BROWNE, Douglas G. and TULLETT, E.V. – Bernard Spilsbury: His Life and Cases (Harrap,1951, reissued 1980)

BURMAN, John – Gleanings from Warwickshire History (Cornish Bros., 1933)

CHADWICK, Owen – The Reformation (Penguin, 1979)

CANNADINE, David – G.M. Trevelyan: a Life in History (Harper Collins, 1992)

COLVILLE, Frederick L. – The Worthies of Warwickshire (Henry T. Cooke, Warwick, 1869)

The Coventry Evening Telegraph

The Daily Telegraph

The Dictionary of National Biography

DILLISTONE, F.W. – C.H. Dodd: Interpreter of the New Testament (Hodder, 1977)

DILLON, Viscount and HOPE, W.H. St. John, eds. – Pageant of the Birth, Life and Death of Richard Beauchamp, Earl of Warwick, K.G., 1389 – 1439 (Longmans, 1914)

DRABBLE, Margaret, and STRINGER, Jenny, eds. – The Concise Oxford Companion to English Literature (O. U. P., 1987)

DRAYTON, Michael – Works, in 5 vols. ed. by J. William Hebel (Shakespeare Head Press, Oxford, 1961)

DUGDALE, William – The Antiquities of Warwickshire (2nd ed., 1730)

EDWARDS, Maldwyn – My Dear Sister: the Story of John Wesley and the Women in His Life (Penwork, 1980)

FABRE, Lucien – Joan of Arc (Odhams, 1954)

FERRY, Georgina – 'The Amazing Dorothy Hodgkin' in Oxford Today, Vol.6, No.3, 1994

FIELD, Jean – She Dyed about Midnight (Brewin Books, 1992)

FIELD, P.J.C. – 'Thomas Malory and the Warwick Retinue Roll' in Midland History, Vol.V, 1979-80, pp.20 – 30.

Focus

GEROULD, Gordon Hall – Sir Guy of Warwick (Harrap, 1914)

The Guardian

HAMILTON, Elizabeth – The Old House at Walton (Michael Russell, 1988)

HARRIS, Mary Dormer – Some Manors, Churches and Villages of Warwickshire (Coventry City Guild, 1937)

HAYDEN, Ruth – Mrs. Delany and Her Flower Collages (British Museum Press, 1992)

HIBBERT, Christopher – The French Revolution (Allen Lane, 1980)

JENNINGS, Christine – Grantchester (Pitkin Pictorials, 1994)

JORDAN, Arthur – The Stratford-upon-Avon and Midland Junction Railway: the Shakespeare Route (Oxford Railway Publishing Company, 1982)

KENDALL, Paul – Warwick the Kingmaker (Allen and Unwin, 1957)

The King's High School, Warwick, 1879 – 1979 (Governing Body, 1979)

LARGE, John Agg – And for Our Next Hymn..., Vols. 1 & 3 (Author, 1 Tawney Croft, Tansley, Matlock, n.d.)

LARKIN, Philip – Collected Poems (Marvell Press, 1988)

Leamington Courier

LONG, Jenny, and BARBER, Andrew – Graciously Pleased: Royal Leamington Spa – 150 Years (Mayneset, 1988)

McINNES, Peter – Randy: the Final, Complete Biography of Randolph Turpin (Caestus Books, 1996)

MARSH, Edward – Rupert Brooke: a Memoir (Sidgwick & Jackson, 1918)

MARTIN, Bernard – An Ancient Mariner: a Biography of John Newton (Wyvern Books, 1960)

MEE, Arthur – Warwickshire (Hodder King's England series, 1936)

The Methodist Recorder

MILLER, Peter – Rupert Brooke (Warwickshire County Council, 1987)

MOSS, Arthur H. – Jerry and Me (unpublished typescript about Billesley, 1975)

MOTION, Andrew – Philip Larkin: a Writer's Life (Faber, 1993)

NEWBOLD, E. B. – Warwickshire History Makers (E. P. Publishing Ltd., 1975)

NICHOLSON, Nora – Chameleon's Dish (Paul Elek, 1973)

The Noble and Renowned History of Guy Earl of Warwick.... (John Merridew, Warwick, 1821)

PALMER, Roy – The Folklore of Warwickshire (Batsford, 1976)

PORTER, Alwyn Francis – A Short History of St. Mary Magdalen Chapel, Guy's Cliffe, Warwick (Guy's Cliffe Masonic Rooms, 2nd. ed., 1989)

PURCELL, William – Onward Christian Soldier: a Life of Sabine Baring-Gould (Longmans, 1957)

RICHMOND, Velma Bourgeois – The Legend of Guy of Warwick (Garland Publishing, 1996)

RIMELL, Mercy – Reflections on Racing, introduced and edited by Ivor Herbert (Pelham, 1990)

ROSS, Michael – Banners of the King: the War of the Vendée, 1793-4 (Hippocrene Books, New York, 1975)

SEVERS, Malcolm – Caroline Bradley: a Tribute (Harrap, 1983)

SEYMOUR, William – Battles in Britain, 1066 – 1547 (Sidgwick & Jackson, 1975)

SHAW, George Bernard – St. Joan (1924)

SHEPARD, Margaret – Princess Olive (P. Drinkwater, Shipston, 1984)

SMITH, Betty – Tales of Old Warwickshire (Countryside Books, Newbury, 1989)

STANSBURY, Don – The Lady who Fought the Vikings (Imogen Books, 1993)

TILLY, Charles – The Vendée (Harvard University Press, 1976)

The Times

TYACK, Geoffrey – Warwickshire Country Houses (Phillimore, 1994)

UGLOW, Jennifer S., *ed.*, – The Macmillan Dictionary of Women's Biography (Macmillan, 1982)

VICKERS, Kenneth H. – England in the Later Middle Ages (Methuen, 1913)

Victoria County History of Warwickshire

WARWICK, Frances Evelyn, Countess of – Warwick Castle and its Earls, Vol. I. (Hutchinson, 1903)

Warwick and Warwickshire Advertiser

Warwickshire and Worcestershire Life

WHELER-GALTON, E. – History of Claverdon (King Stone Press, Long Compton, 1937)

Who Was Who, 1916 – 1928

Who's Who

Acknowledgements

The illustrations of Mrs. Delany's shell work in the text and on the cover are reproduced by courtesy of the Landmark Trust and its photographer Paul Gummer. Copyright remains vested in the Landmark Trust which is a charity renting buildings for self-catering accommodation.

The picture of Philip Larkin and extracts from his poems are reproduced from his "Collected Poems" published by Faber in 1988.

The painting of Henry Tandey carrying a wounded soldier appears by courtesy of Mrs. Cridlan, Norman Parker and the Leamington Courier.

The photograph of Eleanor Doorly appears through the kindness of Miss F. M. Pettle and Jean Field and that of Randolph Turpin by courtesy of Peter McInnes.

Other photographs are by Doreen Bolitho.

Index